# Healing the Haunted

Born in China in 1910, Dr. Kenneth McAll graduated in medicine from Edinburgh University. On his return to China in 1937 his experiences there led to interest in the powers of possession and he has devoted his life since to the curing of psychiatric illness through divine guidance. His unique book on this subject HEALING THE FAMILY TREE (Sheldon Press) has become an international bestseller. It is available from all good bookshops.

His second book THE MOON LOOKS DOWN is a unique illustrated record, with a commentary by his wife, of their gruelling experiences in Japanese internment camps during the Second World War.

He has practised as a Consultant Psychiatrist in England for twenty-five years and is an Associate Member of the Royal College of Psychiatrists.

# HEALING THE HAUNTED

Dr Kenneth McAll

DARLEY ANDERSON
LONDON

First published in Great Britain in 1989 by
Darley Anderson, Estelle House, 11 Eustace Road, London SW6 1JB

ISBN 1 869 838 25 4

Typeset by Inforum Ltd, Portsmouth
Printed and bound in Great Britain by
Anchor Press Ltd, Tiptree, Essex

# Contents

# Introduction

There is a great fascination with ghosts. They titillate our appetite for thrills. For those who actually have to live with ghosts, however, reactions vary from intrigue to terror. Some ghosts rouse no fear and many provide a tourist attraction. Some are much more disturbing.

Haunting can be a serious matter and cause severe disturbance for those who have to endure it. My work over the past ten years has led me to recognise the traumatic effects of past family tragedies and evil on the lives of many people living today. In my first book, *Healing the Family Tree*, I tell of my findings in this field. In addition to the mental upset caused by tragic or evil events in the family history, I have witnessed many cases in which the upset seemed to stem from apparent haunting of a place or house in which the affected person had to live. Some people carry their hauntings with them even though they have moved house especially to escape them.

Not everyone becomes ill as a result of hauntings; but in each case the hauntings create disturbances and often considerable fear. Taking these ghosts and hauntings seriously has meant my trying to identify the individual who is doing the haunting and then treating them as souls in need of help and release. This has been done by holding a service, preferably a Eucharist, on the affected site. And the fact that the hauntings have ceased, and that peace has come to the house or area, and that the affected person has been healed, indicates that we are being successful. Whatever the true explanations of apparitions, they need to be treated, not with fear or mere curiosity, but with respect and compassion.

This book, written at the request of various friends, tells of the stories of these happenings. It also contains one or two stories from my earlier book but here updated and told in greater detail.

# Acknowledgements

The author would like to express his appreciation of the part played by Sheila Richards in several of the recorded events in this book, some of which were initiated by her and others in which she proved an invaluable team-mate.

His thanks are also due to his wife, Dr Frances McAll, his publisher, Darley Anderson and his editor, Mrs Pullen for the help he received from them in the writing of the book.

# The Cavalier

The Cathedral close was barred to traffic at night and no distant sounds reached it. People did not walk about there very late but often at midnight, screaming and yelling, loud thuds and noises were suddenly heard for some time and then just as suddenly they stopped. Tourists, students and staff at the local college were all aware this happened – indeed my research showed that it had been going on for more than three hundred years!

In early Victorian times a tall, red-brick house had been built for the Cathedral staff but now it was a teachers' training college. The residential part of the college was constructed on the site of an ancient nunnery, dating back to the twelfth century, and it was from the attic floor of this building that noises seemed to come. None of the students would sleep in the attic and the atmosphere was cold and eerie. Some of them decided to try an experiment to discover whether the sounds were genuine.

Two simple iron beds were placed there, the floor was uncarpeted and the walls were bare. The students stuck posters on the walls; one was of a bull-fight; one was of Salisbury Cathedral with its beautiful soaring spire; another announced a forthcoming evangelical campaign in London. Strangely, in whatever way the students arranged these posters, every morning they found that the evangelical poster was on the floor while those of the bull-fighter and the Cathedral were never moved. They tried various ways of attaching the posters to the walls but always, in the morning, the same thing happened. One dark, stormy night two students thought they would brave it out and sleep in the room. They said their prayers and went to bed but naturally both remained alert and expectant. As midnight approached, they knelt by their bedsides to pray.

Suddenly without any warning, a tall, dark figure wearing a long black gown and wide-brimmed hat, emerged from the wall cupboard beside the fireplace, without the door opening. He simply came through it. The two students, trembling and fearful, stayed on their knees. Then the figure seemed to be fighting with another person for some time. There were screams and yells followed by silence. Stealthily the tall figure then picked up a body, apparently dead, which he carried through the door and down the stairs. On the way down he dropped the body which rolled to the foot of the stairs. It sounded like a bucket of bricks being emptied. The tall figure then trudged off into the night and silence returned.

The students were absolutely terrified and couldn't sleep. When it was daylight they went to see the College Principal and told her what had happened. She telephoned me and explained the problem so I promised to investigate and see what could be done. A few days later, two Anglican priests and a nurse accompanied me to the college and we all went with the Principal up the stairs to the third floor room where these strange events had supposedly taken place. I opened the door of the wall cupboard, which was a small wardrobe, and found that it led to an attic on the other side of which was a space with access to the roof. The students insisted that the cupboard door had not opened but we were very doubtful, knowing that students have vivid imaginations and enjoy exciting experiences. But we decided to pray together there, in case there really had been some ghostly disturbance. We said, 'Lord Jesus Christ, whatever evil has happened, we are sorry about it and we will hold a proper Eucharistic service here to show forth all that you have provided' and then we repeated the Lord's Prayer.

During the following three weeks we invited interested clergy and church members to take part in a service. On the appointed day we gathered at the college early in the morning – mainly because we did not want publicity or inquisitive tourists to know what was taking place – went up to the room and laid out everything ready for the service. As we were about to start, the Principal asked, 'I wonder if we could have a service of praise and thanksgiving?' I said, 'But we thought you wanted us to hold a Eucharist service here, so that is what we have prepared for.' She replied, 'Well, I don't think we need it because the ghost has never come again since you were last here.' This was an extraordinary surprise because every night at midnight, for over 300 years, the 'haunting' had taken place; then, after we had announced our intention and said the Lord's Prayer, it ceased!

According to legend, a Cavalier had apparently come over the roof tops and entered a nun's room where he had raped and killed her and then carried off her body. Presumably he dropped her on the way down the stairs which would account for the noise of falling. The Principal maintained, however, that events did not happen in this way, for the noise did not begin in the room but in the space above the road outside the building where, in fact, the Nunnery used to stand. We suggested that we should try to retrace the footsteps of this man, repeating the Lord's Prayer as we went. Some people have an innate sensitivity to such situations and the nurse who was with us was one of these people. She felt that there was a cold shiver in the atmosphere which she could follow and which would indicate to her the way the Cavalier had gone. At the bottom of the stairs, therefore, we walked along a stone-flagged corridor at the end of which we turned right into a hallway. But at that point, according to the nurse, all the vibrations suddenly stopped.

In the hallway, students' coats were hanging on racks and hangers and the floor was covered by thick rubber squares. I asked the Principal whether this building had any cellars and she was quite sure that there were none. 'But,' I insisted, 'by tapping the floor where we are standing now I can tell that this is a wooden floor so there must be some space underneath.' She repeated that there were no cellars so I asked whether we could push the coat racks to one side and pull up the rubber squares and have a look. She agreed and when we did this we found a trap door in the floor with an old brass ring handle inset. We heaved it up and discovered steps going down into a corridor below which had been blocked off a little way along by a back wall. We decided that this must be where the Cavalier took the nun's body.

Some days later, the Principal again telephoned to thank us for our efforts and assure us that everything was now peaceful. It seemed strange to us that nothing had been done about the situation before, because from the site of this dreadful happening one could see straight across the lawns to the front entrance of the Cathedral. Had no one ever heard the sounds? Did they never try to do anything about it? And why not? People do not realise that it is a very simple process to release such lost souls, who are earthbound and who are repeating over and over again, the way they died or what they had done wrong; perhaps bemoaning their own guilt, and trying to draw attention to it.

People are frightened by such ghosts and run away and do not try to help them. But we are able to do much by displaying to the forces of evil in the Eucharist service, all that our Lord accomplished so that these lost souls can finally leave their earthbound state and start on the journey to Heaven.

4

# The Smugglers

In one Diocese of the Church of England the Bishop, who was very much opposed to my ideas, had never allowed his clergy to hold exorcism services. This meant that we had to carry the consecrated bread and wine from my own nearby church to the haunted site and take a service with the local clergyman.

One place we went to was a hotel which was haunted at night by the strange muffled noises of men fighting. The hotel guests were put up on the first and second floors because of these disturbances, but the owners themselves slept on the ground floor nearest to the place from which the noises emanated. Despite this, guests upstairs occasionally ran out of their rooms screaming that they would never go back there again, because of what they had heard. The four members of the owner's family always slept together in the same room so that they could support each other during the night.

I was invited to deal with the situation and the local clergyman and I made some enquiries. Neighbours told us that they thought the noise came from underneath the hotel and there were many old smugglers' tunnels running from the coast up to the town, probably beneath the hotel and the public houses. They told us that no-one knew where the tunnels' openings were but they were quite sure that this hotel stood above one of the places where smugglers used to bring their goods.

It seemed likely that there might have been fights and even killings before the place had been abandoned. Naturally, no one would have prayed for the victims, so we placed two candles on a small tea-table and set out the bread and the wine and held a Eucharist service for them in the hotel.

As a result complete peace ensued and the hotel owners were extremely grateful.

# The Miner's Lamp

Recently I was called again to the same Diocese this time by the Bishop himself. He asked me to return because of a complaint about a haunted house near to where he lived. The local vicar had previously requested permission to carry out a service there but, as the Bishop had never allowed anyone to do so, this had still not been done. The Bishop now asked me to help conduct the service with the vicar.

It was an ordinary little terraced house with the stairs coming down to the front door and a passage on the right, leading to a bedroom, sitting room and kitchen. We sat down with the lady of the house and asked her what had been happening. She told us that with gradually increasing frequency over the years she had been awakened at night, usually at about two o'clock in the morning, by the sound of drilling which grew louder and louder and recently had become so loud that it sounded like a pneumatic drill. It seemed to come from beneath the floor of the hallway and, at the same time, a very bright light like a spot-light travelled around the bedroom walls.

At first the lady thought that her neighbours were doing 'home improvements' in the night, or that road works were being carried out but investigations and questioning established that the noise and the light were not heard by anyone else – even the next door neighbours had heard nothing.

The lady was however terrified. Some nights her son had to come and stay with her because she was so scared of sleeping alone in her own home. Her son unsuccessfully investigated all possible sources of the 'spot-light'. How, we wondered, could it get in from the outside through closed curtains and travel around her room? We thought that perhaps it might have come down the hall from the road or from a burglar's torch but it could not permeate the closed front door and even the door under the stairs, which would normally block its access, didn't do so.

As we talked with the lady about her family and drew out a Family Tree, we discussed the life of her elder brother, a coalminer, who had died many years before. I asked about his funeral and the way that he had died. She said there had been no funeral as his body had never been found. It seemed clear then that the man had been underground, drilling for coal with his miner's lamp strapped to his helmet, shining ahead of him. He was trying to draw attention to the way in which he had died and was only repeating his last memories. I suggested that we should hold a service for her brother and as a result her troubles ceased.

# The Old Witch

Deep in the English countryside in a village dominated by a church with a spire, thatched and timbered cottages line a narrow winding road. One of them had been modernised and a wing added, in keeping with the old style, but obviously new brickwork had to be used. A family had come to live in this cottage, to enable the father to be near his work. In one area of the newly built wing, which was now the kitchen, the meters for the electricity, water mains and central heating were housed; but the great problem was that one after another each of these utilities failed to work. No sooner had the electrician or the plumber or the boiler man been to repair the appropriate system than one of the other systems would go wrong again. This situation went on and on.

When I visited this family we sat quietly and considered why this should be happening in one particular area as nothing else was wrong in the rest of the house. We thought about earlier times when the cottage was built and realised that the kitchen doorway, which led into the rest of the house, was once the front door. We also realised that this end of the house was on the main crossing of the village, perhaps ten feet above the road, and we conjectured that in the past the occupier would sit outside the front door under the heavily thatched eaves, watching people going up and down the road. Then we pictured an old woman sitting there who had been involved with witchcraft and who started putting curses on people. When she died, she was regarded as a witch. Acting on this assumption, we decided to hold a service on the exact spot where she would have sat cursing the passers-by, in case she was still wandering about and feeling very angry about the alterations to her cottage. We prayed for her and, amazingly, the disturbance did not occur again and all the apparatus functioned normally.

# Shaggy Dog

A professional man and his family had moved into a new house only to find that they were disturbed at night by a dog running up and down the two flights of stairs and bounding from landing to landing. Their impression was of a big shaggy dog. The consequent thuds and heavy breathing were terrifying and naturally kept them awake. Although we did not know the reason for this we decided to hold a service in the house. After this the family, the dog and the house were all at peace.

Some years later, when a part of the house was being altered, a large old-fashioned water radiator situated in front of a deep bay window had to be removed. Behind it, right into the recess of the window and previously covered by a window-seat, was a large space where they discovered two candlesticks, hieroglyphics on the wall and an outline of a dog lying on the ground. The owners presumed that a witchcraft ceremony had taken place there and confirmed the idea that there was a dog trying to command our attention.

The question of whether 'dogs go to Heaven' has concerned many dog lovers. Once during a Eucharist service we saw (in our visual imagery) an unknown person, like an old shepherd with his dog. He came sadly down the aisle with his head bowed to kneel at the altar. His dog beside him looked equally depressed with a droopy tail and his head down. They were allowed to witness the service but, as it finished, they rose and the shepherd walked sprightly off into the very bright light with the angel guardians and his dog happily following behind him, his big white tail swinging from side to side as they disappeared.

# The Church Cleaner

Once, when I had been lecturing in Norfolk, I stayed overnight in a village vicarage with friends of mine. In the morning I visited the nearby church, small, old and beautiful. I was sitting there quietly when all of a sudden, there was a lot of talking and the sounds of a bucket and water being used and of general cleaning. At first I took no notice, thinking that it was just the cleaner working near the pulpit. After a while, and because the noise seemed to be very persistent, I walked to the pulpit expecting to see someone cleaning behind it. Rounding the corner alongside the pulpit steps all I found was a blank wall! I turned, presuming that there must be a passage way leading into the vestry, but again there was just a blank wall with an engraved brass plate on it. With a shock I realised that at that moment all the noises ceased. Collecting myself, I walked back to the vicarage and told the vicar about the incident. He was very glad that I could verify this happening because he and other people had been similarly troubled and had tried to dismiss it as imaginary. As a stranger, I had witnessed it without having heard about it.

Obviously we had to do something about the situation, assuming that some cleaner had died near the pulpit and possibly had no memorial of any kind. It certainly could not be the well-known name on the brass plate. In case the person had not been committed to God, we held a Eucharistic service at the altar steps and prayed for who ever this person was. After that there was no recurrence of the disturbing noises in the church.

# The Image in the Dust

Opposite a London church was a large stone Victorian building which was due to be renovated and made into a centre for the church's use. Because of the excessive dust, the builders had to wear masks while removing the plaster facing which was hiding the beautiful red brickwork beneath. Many of the workmen refused to work on the wide stairways of the building because they were frequently frightened by the sight of the outline of a young woman in the dusty air. On making enquiries, it was discovered that a young girl had hung herself on the staircase many years before. So we held a service for her. As we did not know the girl's name, we invented one to make the situation more real.

She was never seen again.

# The Services and Satan

I was called to a military base by the Deputy Commander because various strange incidents were happening to people there. I was specifically asked to see the Chaplain, who had been arrested by the Military Police.

Two little girls had accused him of spanking them during

a Sunday school lesson, so the police were bound to investigate. The Chaplain was put under house arrest for five days and could not continue his pastoral duties, an extremely humiliating situation for him. I was asked to write a report on whether there were any grounds at all for the allegations against him. I discovered that the children were taught at school that Satan could destroy people. Some months earlier, a group who did not like their RE teacher, had ganged together and reported him to their Headmaster, accusing him of mishandling girls in class. The Headmaster advised the man of the situation and told him that it would be a police matter to ascertain whether he was guilty of misbehaviour or not. If, however, the teacher left the school immediately and his whereabouts were unknown, then the Headmaster would not be able to do anything about it. Also, if he took a job out of the area before the story became common knowledge, he would probably be safe. The teacher agreed and left. The same girls, whose parents were on the staff of the base then switched their attention to the Chaplain.

At about the same time, a light aeroplane carrying the Commander of the base back from Europe suddenly plummeted out of the sky and both he and the pilot were killed. Investigations into the crash proved negative; no error of judgement could be proven; no electrical fault could be found and the weather was normal. The bodies were retrieved and brought back to the base to be laid out in the Chapel. By the time the undertakers had finished their work it was early morning. The Chaplain, who still had the key to the Chapel, was taken across under escort. When the doors were opened it was discovered, to everyone's horror, that the Chapel that night must have been used for a witchcraft coven. The alter crucifix and the bible were upside down. The altar cloth had cigarette ash and stubs all over it; chairs had been turned upside down and obviously a group of people had been around the altar. It was apparent that it was a witches' coven and not just youths fooling around, because it was highly organised with reversal procedures of everything classed as holy. It was most disconcerting. Investigations showed that some people on the base were experimenting with spiritualism and others were playing with ouija boards and delving into the occult. There was also trouble concerning wife-swapping and additionally there was a small Communist group who were causing a lot of disruption. There was also friction between the ranks. One man had dressed himself as a high ranking officer, pretending to be from another base and had been arrested when using the Officers Mess.

These incidents were all happening at the same time and the problem was how to sort it out. Satan the arch enemy and maker of lies was using people, like puppets, to disrupt the life of the place. The Medical Officer was both keen and extremely helpful to me in my investigations, arranging interviews and organising visits to various places. In some cases I found tremendous opposition and cynicism but on the whole the patterns fitted together very well. There seemed to be very little actual spiritual discipline and because of their low standards of behaviour people had opened themselves to unfounded accusations and disruptions. It was possible that the witchcraft coven had actually caused the destruction of the Commander – some of the lower ranks were antagonistic towards him – by willing his aeroplane to crash out of the sky. (Such a thing has happened before, as described in Doreen Irwin's book *From Witchcraft to Christ*). A team of Christian people gathered together on the base and prayed about these complicated problems.

On the day of the Chaplain's Court Martial, five beribboned officers sat in a row at the front with the defence and prosecution counsels sitting at tables on either side. Then began the long case for the prosecution, the two little girls being the main witnesses. They were to tell their stories out of earshot from one another, fortunately, because their evidence was contradictory. The second day of the trial was drawn out and involved. An officer asked one of the girls, who was about twelve years old, how she knew so much about sexual matters and that it was naughty to have her bottom spanked by someone else. She embroidered her story to describe how the Chaplain had taken her to his bedroom and raped her. She was so knowledgeable that the presiding officer asked her whether this had ever happened to her before. The child then slowly turned around and looked around her before turning to face him again. He asked her why she had turned round to search the courtroom and the child replied that she just wanted to check whether her father was present. Having established that he was not there, the officer asked why it mattered. The child said, 'I promised Daddy I would not tell.' Told to explain, she said that when she was eight years old, her father, pretending to be a burglar, had come into her bedroom and raped her. She had learned the details then from him.

This girl's fabrications had been so extensive that the other child could not confirm any of her story. The examining officers decided there was no case to answer and that the charge was without foundation. The case was dismissed without any defence being called. On the following Sunday there was an enormous response from the base and, for the first time, the church was full for a service of rejoicing. A Bible study group was set up and the future looked promising. There was thankfulness that there had been a victory for truth and a general moral clean-up.

Six months later, however, the Chaplain was told to report to H.Q. where he was asked to resign from the service and given a few months' notice. The reason given was that there had been too much 'tittle tattle' about what had happened and it had to be stopped before it spread to other camps. The matter was not to be pursued any further. There was a short cover-up story in the newspapers at the time and eventually the base itself was abandoned.

# Peter the Tramp

Mary was very distressed. On yet another night her husband had not come home. It was 3 o'clock in the morning and imagining that he must again be with another prostitute the familiar pain in her stomach of depression and rejection tore her apart. She felt that there was no escape from her misery. It was a warm, still night so Mary suddenly decided to go out with no idea of where she was going; just needing to get away. Her children, who were in their late 'teens, were asleep in bed. Wearing only a dressing-gown over her nightdress and slippers on her feet she found herself walking down a pathway beside the canal bank near her house. Many years before it had been used by horses to tug the barges and was now overgrown and weedy. Mary determined that, in this silent, lonely place, she would end it all by drowning herself. Absorbed in her thoughts she was startled when a dishevelled old man, in torn clothes, stepped out of the bushes in front of her on the pathway. He held up his hand. 'No, don't do it this way, go home again,' he said in a friendly voice. Mary stood still staring at him. He repeated, 'Go home, this isn't the way.' Wearily she turned and dragged herself back home to bed and to sleep.

A few days later she was sitting alone in her house when there was a knock on the door. She opened it to find the same old man, who had appeared on that bewildering night standing there in the same dirty old clothes. She invited him in and offered him tea and food. He refused them but sat down and began to talk very gently to her and Mary found him both kind and understanding.

The next week, as she was tidying her bedroom, the old man walked into the house again, sat down and spoke to her very gently about her troubles, assuring her that there was a way out and that she would be able to find the answer although he did not explain how. On another occasion Mary's son came home unexpectedly and bounded into the house, whereupon the old man, according to her, rushed down the stairs and out of the front door. Her son, rather alarmed, shouted, 'Who was that and what is he doing here?' as the shadowy figure fled away. Mary said she did not know what he was talking about. Several times similar events happened. Mary became disturbed because she thought the old tramp must have been hungry and thirsty but he would never accept food or drink from her. She also noticed, that despite being torn and tattered, he did not smell at all. He was just peaceful and kindly.

Finally, she took her son into her confidence and one day when he heard her talking to a man in the sitting room he burst in upon them. There was nobody there – except his mother. He was terrified and rushed out to the nearby church but found it locked. He hammered on the door. Most disturbing was the fact that his face and body towards the church door felt very hot but his back, facing away from the door, felt icy cold. He found the vicar's name from the church notice board beside the door and quickly went to see him in great distress to ask him to go to his mother as something was evidently wrong. The vicar accompanied him to his house but all seemed peaceful there. When he tried to find out from Mary what the trouble was she was quite unable and unwilling to tell him. Some days later, the vicar suggested that I should see her. She told me that she had heard that the towpath by the river was haunted and people would never walk there at night because often an old man had been seen. Mary had learned from the old man, who visited her frequently, that his name was Peter, so from then on he became known as Peter the Tramp.

The local vicar, a neighbouring vicar and I, and some of Mary's family, decided that we would hold a Communion service in the parish church to pray for Peter's release from whatever he had done in life, so that this family could be unified again.

Regrettably we could not pray aloud for Mary's husband's behaviour with other women as he would not admit to it; perhaps, in his heart he might have made his apologies to God.

When we left the church I suggested that we all walked to the pathway alongside the canal bank so that we could pray at the actual site where the old man Peter had first appeared. Several other people joined us, wanting to experience this journey and to pray with us; so about twelve of us set off. Mary told us when we had reached the place. We bowed our heads and prayed; some of us praying for Satan to be defeated and for Peter to be forgiven. Suddenly, to my amazement, in my mind's eye, I saw a figure rise up from out of the water. He wore a white gown and his arms were outstretched and extended towards us. He said, 'Thank you for what you are doing'. I was puzzled by the fact that this rather beautiful youth looked so young and I said aloud, 'I can see Peter, he is about 18 years old and he is going up to Heaven'. Mary, who had also seen Peter said, 'Yes, that's right, when he was about that age he disobeyed God and finally as an old man he drowned here in the canal, now he is allowed to go back to the beginning with forgiveness and to start life all over again in his new body.'

It was very exciting and interesting. Peace descended upon the family and the area and Peter has never appeared again. We know this because we followed up the investigation for several years through the vicar, who lived close by.

# The Garden of Cats

The terrifying spectre of a young woman curled up at the back of a huge open fireplace in an English country house hissing and spitting and clawing at anyone who came near to her was most distressing. When this happened her family had to leave her lying there until she temporarily recovered. And this had happened many times.

It was a very large, old stone house and in this room the fireplace was staged by ironwork to retain the enormous logs and to prevent them from falling onto the flagstone. The mantelpiece itself was six feet in height and the whole opening six feet wide. It was a cold, unpleasant, unfurnished room with a high ceiling and vast windows, now used only as a dumping room. It was too big to heat and too uncomfortable to sit in. It had now become a frightening room into which the children would never go.

I was asked whether I could help. The garden, which clearly had been very beautiful and well-kept, almost manicured, with box hedges and rows of patterned flower beds, was now overgrown. It seemed to me rather unpleasant that in many corners of this garden there were memorial tablets to cats, with their names, birth dates and death dates – about thirty or forty of them positioned at random. Apparently, some previous inhabitants of the house had devoted their lives to cats.

We could only conjecture as to what had occurred. Perhaps some angry servant, tired of burying yet another animal, had thrown a dead cat on to the large wood-burning fire. Perhaps, even, an aborted or miscarried human foetus had been similarly discarded, without a proper burial service.

We sat with the family in their warm sitting room and there prayed together, committing the whole situation to God and apologising for whatever cruel deeds had been done in the abandoned room. The family promised that they would attend the local church and apologise to God in a Eucharistic service.

Their mother's strange behaviour never happened again and the house is now at peace.

# The Ashes in the Pulpit

Whenever visiting clergymen went to one particular church, they would naturally go into the pulpit to preach. They would walk up the steps to the pulpit and then immediately come down again and stand at the chancel steps to preach their sermons. Even the church's own vicar would never read, or preach, or even speak from this pulpit because it held an extraordinarily unpleasant feeling.

Most disturbing was that the first thing you saw in the pulpit was a little brass plate on which was inscribed, 'Here are scatted the ashes of the Reverend Smith.' This man had been a very famous preacher in his day but when he retired to the other end of the British Isles he became involved in the occult. I had been asked to visit him, when he was in his eighties, because he was extremely depressed. I, and several colleagues, spent an afternoon with him, trying in vain to break through his depression and to warn him of the dangers of the occult. He reacted angrily to all this however, refusing to pray with us, and he was especially angry with me for daring to interfere. We parted on very bad terms. I wrote to him but received a rude reply. He died a very lonely man.

Strangely, when I was called to the investigation of this church, I found that it was the same man whose ashes had been scattered over the pulpit and the brass plate affixed at his request in his will.

We held a service in the church, with a small group of concerned people, to apologise to God, on Mr Smith's behalf, for all wrong doing. And we prayed that he might understand both the forgiveness that we were showing forth in the bread and wine and the new life which was available to him.

It must have been more than the healing of our memories which had occurred at that service. From then on, to the great delight of the vicar, visiting clergy who knew nothing of the history of this pulpit were now able to use it naturally without encountering any disturbance or unpleasantness.

# London Bridge

The teenage daughter of an English family, who had emigrated, wanted to return to Britain to study. She was a well-balanced and capable girl, but while she was staying in London she had very disturbed nights. She could hear scratching noises around her and the sound of deep breathing. To escape these disturbances she moved accommodation – but the noises still continued in exactly the same way. Moreover, the closer she was to a particular bridge the more disturbed she became. She grew more and more depressed and a friend brought her to see me.

Having listened to her story we drew up a Family Tree. We found that an aunt had committed suicide in London by jumping over a bridge and because all the family had been abroad at the time, no one had attended the funeral service. The relatives had never thought about having a service of their own. It was a simple solution to hold a service for the aunt; to apologise and commit her to God and, by doing so, to end the teenager's troubles.

It was strange, however, that these events should occur only when the girl moved to London and I wondered why the relatives abroad were not disturbed by this aunt. Had she perhaps waited until someone from the family came to the actual place where she had died? The lapse of time and distance in this area of eternity is not as we measure them on earth.

I have been in contact with the family for over ten years since these events took place and there has been no further disturbance.

# The Pirates and the Chinese

Two Chinese lady doctors spent some time at Galveston in Texas to complete their training; each specialised in a different branch of medicine. Galveston on the Mexican Gulf, seventy-five miles south of Houston, is an island now joined to the mainland by a road-bridge. It is a very long sand bar lined with houses and is gradually being reclaimed by the sea.

The Chinese ladies lived at the far east end of the spit of land where there were mostly fishing shacks mounted upon stilts and at night it was a deserted and lonely area. The Chinese mentality is attuned to previous generations, and so the doctors felt uneasy because they knew that pirates had used these shores as a landing place in earlier times.

When they returned to China, where I met them, they still felt disturbed about the area they had left. Together, we drew out a Family Tree and found that one of them was of Japanese Samurai descent on her mother's side. Samurais are very proud people with fighting rituals, conquering attitudes and sword ceremonials. We learned that sometimes in the warring between the princes, all the relatives including sons, young girls and old people would be executed, except for just one girl. This girl would be saved to start a new family and to continue the line and people were proud of this tradition. The doctor felt very ashamed about this behaviour, so she took it to God and was absolutely delighted by the release she receiced from worry, tension and depression which her awareness of the Galveston pirates had triggered off.

The two doctors had a Buddhist servant girl who often complained about being kept awake at night by her best friend, a girl who had committed suicide by paraquat poisoning. She joined very willingly in one of our Eucharistic services and repeated the necessary words we thought she should say; she herself had no understanding or experience of this kind of service. Next day, however, she complained to her mistress that the service had not made any difference and that she had again had a very bad night. The following night she was still very disturbed. But in the morning when she looked out of her window at a dry fish pond in the garden she saw a branch of a rose bush spring up from the middle of the pond. At the very top of the bush was an extremely beautiful red rose. She watched for a long time and then withdrew to start work, telling her mistress about this omen of 'good' which she had witnessed.

22

We decided to hold another service with her because, when we drew up a Family Tree of her best friend, we discovered that not only had her friend's Mother also committed suicide by paraquat poisoning but her Grandfather had apparently done the same thing. The tragedy was being repeated generation after generation. In the second service, therefore, the girl said her prayers again and this time included her friend's Mother and Grandfather. The next morning she reported that she had slept well. Subsequent nights were peaceful and she asked to be baptized as a Christian and was extremely happy.

# The Coffin Ships

I have in my possession a picture of an old wooden sailing ship anchored in Weymouth harbour. Flying from the mast is the New Zealand flag and on its side a large notice saying 'Convict Ship'. It was these ships, often called 'coffin ships', which transported convicted criminals to the other side of the world in the eighteenth and nineteenth centuries; criminals often convicted of no more than debt, minor theft or, like the Tolpuddle martyrs, simply for meeting together in groups of more than six. They were herded together, sometimes in chains and many died from terrible conditions on their six months voyage.

Those who survived came under strict and often cruel military authority. The military personnel were as cut off from their home country as the convicts and were only too ready to vent their frustrations on the convicts. One of the jobs given to the convicts under the direction of the Governor, was to go out into the countryside to hunt and kill the local Aborigines. Later, when the convicts completed their sentences and became settlers, 'Abo hunting' became a favourite sport amongst them.

When I visited Brisbane, I stayed with the granddaughter of one of these cruel Governors. She was very ashamed of all that had happened in the past, particularly the flogging and hanging given as punishment to the miserable convicts. Not only did those who were there suffer cruelty but so did men from the neighbouring countries of New Guinea and the Pacific Islands who were rounded up and brought over to do the heavy, hot work in the plantations with promises of good housing, food and clothes. Many just worked till they died as they had no means of escape. This practice was called 'black-birding'.

While I was there, an elderly couple brought their son to me. He was about thirty years old and a very large, tough man. He walked with his legs apart, with a macho cowboy swagger and his big, sloping shoulders hid enormous strength. He was much feared throughout the area because, when he became very angry, he just smashed up whatever was nearest to him. He had also written off more than a hundred cars in accidents. His father told me he had been violent ever since he was young and that his grandfather had been the same.

I asked where this had started in the Family Tree but all that his father knew was that some very minor offence had been committed in a London street by one of his ancestors who had subsequently been put on a convict ship. Presumably the man had been extremely angry when he arrived in Australia and had vented his wrath on all and sundry. Now one man, in each succeeding generation of this family, was behaving in the same way. This man's son knew he had a problem which he was totally unable to control.

I suggested that we should come together to God to apologise for man's cruelty to man through the ages and the son agreed that this would be a good idea. He had already seen evidence of change in other people who had experienced this service. Our prayers were spoken aloud and the son insisted that his mother should say them because he trusted her. She was very willing and it seemed that at the moment when she promised to do so, this tough man relaxed and the pressure was lifted off him. Following the actual service, there was great peace and joy in the family – especially for his young wife!

# Aborigines

Many years ago, four brothers settled in Australia, taking over a large area of land. The local Aborigines, enraged by this, murdered one of the brothers. In revenge for this murder, the other three brothers went out and shot four Aborigines. A descendant of the brothers felt this crime very deeply and longed to put things right. He and his wife went to the area, where they believed it had happened, and found that the incident was well remembered and the very spot where the Aborigines had been killed was also known. That evening they went and prayed over the place asking for God's forgiveness.

The following morning in the nearby town, the young husband saw an elderly Aborigine sitting at the wheel of a parked car so asked him what tribe had originally lived in those parts. The Aborigine, wanting to know why he was interested in this, invited him to join him in the car and the young man found himself pouring out the whole story and his longing for forgiveness and reconciliation.

The older man's response was immediate. 'I too love the

Lord Jesus,' he said, and told how he had spent his life ministering to his people in that area. He said he was sure that God forgave them all and that he, himself, was certainly ready to forgive. Together, in the car, they prayed. Since then, many friendships have sprung up between the white family and Aboriginal families in that area and when I was in a town on the other side of the country, I heard this story being repeated by an Aboriginal pastor.

Several months later, the young man's father attended a Eucharist at which he too apologised to God for the killing of Aborigines by his ancestors. At the end of the service, he came to the front to tell the two hundred or so people there, how, during the service he had had a clear vision of many 'brown-skinned men' going joyfully up to Heaven.

# The Level Crossing

A young professional friend was becoming progressively more depressed. She had not responded to prescribed anti-depressants nor was the pattern of her illness at all typical. On drawing out her Family Tree, we found that her mother had had a miscarriage many years before. As her mother was rather infirm and did not want to go out, the local vicar and I went to their house to hold a straightforward service and offered prayers in every room. My young friend told me that she felt very much better afterwards but she was surprised by the cessation of an annoying occurrence which had always puzzled them. From the chimney-piece of their sitting-room a loud rattling noise had always emanated. They had tried remedies such as blocking up the chimney breast, dispensing with a coal fire, changing to a gas fire, and then to an electric fire but all to no avail: the rattling noises had continued. Draught controls and double glazing were also tried and roofing repairs were carried out. But the noises had not stopped. Then, after we held the service, the noises did stop.

My friend also told us that at the bottom of their garden there was a railway which ran over a level crossing. Once, there had been a disaster, when a derailed train had run straight through the garden beside the level crossing and through the crossing keeper's house, killing all its occupants. When the rescue work was completed and the bodies removed, the six-year old son could not be found. He was never traced and so he never had a burial service.

Perhaps, in our service beside the crossing, we had shown forth what should have happened to the little boy; perhaps it was he who was knocking at the chimney-piece through the years, trying to attract attention; perhaps he had waited until he found sensitive people in the house whom he could trust. This is the only explanation we can offer. From the day of our service, the knocking in the chimney was never heard again.

# Ship's Timbers

A happy, united family lived in an old, thatched cottage but often they felt very disturbed there: they had a strong feeling of someone 'intruding'. The mother was home most of the time and could not understand these peculiar disturbances and the sensations she felt, so she asked me to visit them. I noticed that the beautiful huge oak beams spanning the ceiling of the sitting room were gnarled and shaped: they were obviously old ship's timbers. Often, when ships were old and no longer seaworthy, they were dismantled and the main deck beams utilised for building cottages, and these timbers occasionally retained remnants of bolt holes and burn marks. Sometimes these ships had been involved in fighting battles against the French or Spanish, and then towed back to Britain and their timbers re-used.

We studied their Family Tree and found that ancestors could not be accounted for. While talking about this, the family said that an old man had sometimes been seen on the stairs. He was not terrifying, but it was still a little alarming because he just appeared and then quietly disappeared up the stairs. They said he looked more like a countryman than a seaman. We held a service there. Exactly what we released we do not know but since then everything has been happy and peaceful and the disturbed atmosphere in the house has disappeared. Perhaps one of the missing family members was released. Certainly the old man has never appeared again.

# The Farmer

I visited a new housing estate which had been built on rather beautiful farming land. A sensitive family had moved into one of these houses and the parents were disturbed because their children had often seen a white-gowned figure walking about. The children described the gown as being rather like a smock made of rough material and gathered around the waist. The figure wore heavy boots and walked very angrily through the estate as though the houses and gardens did not exist. The parents were alarmed because, apparently, the figure would go right through the walls, striding with his head down and ignoring everything around him.

We all sat together in the house and tried to imagine what was causing this and our thoughts were channelled to a farmer of an earlier generation who was angry about what had happened to his land. He had spread manure, cut hay, mended hedges, and delighted in the greenness and abundance of the pastures through which his contented cows sauntered. Then he had watched helplessly as his land was invaded by bulldozers, drainage pipes, sewers and redbrick houses and all his work destroyed. We agreed that he must have been a man who had died very unhappily.

We held a service for him and afterwards all was peaceful. It is easy to write that 'all was peaceful afterwards,' but during the last few years, this family has indeed been peaceful and there has been no reappearance of the farmer.

When people move to a new house it is a good idea to have it blessed. I would go further and include prayers for the whole area in a Eucharist as there may be other lost souls still wandering about and needing help and committal to God.


# Doors and Windows

I was called to see a very brave lady who was dying of cancer. She was a delightful person, quite active and not on sedatives, but perfectly aware that her time was short. In the few weeks prior to sending for me, she had been alarmed because sometimes, during the day or night, the outer doors of her house would be flung open and windows would fly outwards on their hinges, in spite of the locks and bolts.

It was a most puzzling and disturbing situation. If burglars had been responsible, how were the doors opened without breaking the locks? How were the upstairs bedroom windows opened even in occupied rooms? And why was nothing stolen? I wandered around the house trying to find the answers to these questions and asked other people who had stayed there whether they had been able to open the doors and windows from the outside. Some were strangely annoyed at being questioned; some had an explanation. We checked the lady's Family Tree but could find nothing wrong; she was a very good person. Finally, we asked a local clergyman to hold a Eucharistic service in the house for whomever or whatever was troubled. It was a very happy service during which the dying lady joined in prayer. Shortly afterwards she became bedridden and died a few days later. But she died very happily and the house has been peaceful ever since.

# Cave Men

In a southern part of Britain's coast, deep dark woods covered a hillside. On the crown of the hill, several hundred feet high, was a bare rock in the centre of which was a depression which formed a natural fortification and defence position. It had been used as such for generations, because from the top you could see for many miles around.

The dark oak woods of enormous trees covered several acres and were always very cold but not damp. The extreme coldness seemed to be attributed more to one's own sensation about the area than the actual temperature and the place was disliked. Many times people had the feeling that their sleeves were being plucked by someone behind them but, on turning round, there was never anybody there. On the higher parts of the woodland there were very tall rocks, some of them six or eight feet high, covered with ferns and separated by deep pits. I felt that someone there was trying to attract attention and realized that these rocks would have been natural caves for Stone Age people.

We decided that it would be right to hold a Eucharist service there for whoever was haunting the place. So in a sunny glade where a gentle breeze made the shadows dance on the brown dry leaves below, we set out a little table and chairs. Nearby was the home of a family who loved the area and they joined us. Their cat as usual bounded along, rushing here and there with his tail held high. When they came to the glade, however, the cat would not approach anywhere near it but crawled up to the top of the rocks to sit and stare at us from under a fern. Strangely, the cat would crawl down the side of one rock and then climb up and sit on the top of another one, glaring at us from under the ferns. All the time he kept well within a radius of about twenty-five feet.

We started our prayers with the Lord's Prayer and we were aware of a plucking sensation at our sleeves. One person suddenly said, 'She's pinching my cheeks!' 'Who's she?' I asked. 'A little brown old lady,' was the reply 'filthy and dishevelled, wearing a tattered muddy skin. She looks very puzzled.' We realised that any cave dwellers would not know who we were or what we were doing there. They were pulling at our clothes, presumably wondering what we wore and pinching our white cheeks as though we were statues, clearly wondering what sort of creatures we were. We could see more such people hiding behind trees and others approaching from a distance. There were many of them: the men bearded and all very dirty and muddy with matted hair. They seemed inquisitive and some crept near on their hands and knees. We continued with our service, thinking that we were showing them what Jesus Christ had done for all men both in the world that had passed, and in our present world and in the world of the future.

Then, creeping through the woods further down the hill came men who looked rather like buccaners, dressed in striped shirts with handkerchiefs around their heads and carrying cutlasses. Obviously, they came from another age altogether and nearer to ours than the stoneage. The different groups of people seemed unaware of each other and passed through each other. Probably, this group were Spanish seamen bent on capturing the headland, probably at the time of the Armada.

Then appeared taller, disciplined men, in bright red jackets, with blue trousers and tri-cornered hats, carrying old-fashioned muskets with long bayonets. Among them walked a Roman Catholic priest with a big white cross on his dark brown habit. His tonsured head seemed to lean backwards as if he were unwilling to be part of the soldiers. They seemed to be French. On seeing us in the glade, they came abruptly to a halt and stared as we showed forth to them the bread and the wine. We went slowly and reverently through our service, aware that all these people were watching us. At the end of the service, as we gave the final blessing, a remarkable thing happened. The cat jumped off its pinnacle, came down and sat on my knee, then went onto other people's knees and finally rolled on to its back, purring, under the table that we had used. As people were released by our service to start their journey towards Heaven, so the cat watched them go and was able to come into the circle of sunlight.

A few days later, as we walked through the woods, we still felt cold but there was no plucking at our sleeves. When we thought about the people whom we had seen, we realised that the Spanish and the French had heard of Jesus Christ and would know what we were talking about and understand what we were showing them. They moved away after the service, unlike the cave people, who were stoneage people and who did not know our language and probably had no idea what we were doing or what we were showing. How could they understand our service? They did not go away but stayed gawking at us. We decided that it would be right to go back to the woods each day and read aloud to them from the Bible. We chose St. Matthew's Gospel and we found it to be rather a pleasant experience. The very trees seemed to be listening, the huge oaks and beeches standing like pillars in a cathedral with their tall branches meeting above in a canopy of green. When the readings were finished, the whole sensation in the woods was different, friendlier and warmer. There was no more plucking or pinching and it was pleasant and relaxing to walk there.

# Studley Castle

After having had the previous experience in the woods, we went to Studley Castle, which is also hidden in a forest and used a metal detector. We found a thirty foot square gravel bank rising to no more than three feet on any side but located on a promontory of land within the forest. It was surprising that the metal detector picked up nothing at all as I expected that there would be at least a few rusty nails! Then I realised that this castle dated from a much earlier date. It probably only had a wooden pallisade with mud huts inside, not as protection from invaders but from the wild animals that roamed the forest in those days. Searching then in the gravel itself, we discovered a flint axe and many flint chips.

We then tried to recreate the original scene in our mind. We knew that the people would have had little means of communication with each other. In visual imagery we saw, at the entrance to the place, a man with a stone-headed shaft tucked into his skins. He was old and shaggy and bearded and stood as a sort of guardian. There were women moving around and staring at us, the strange, modern intruders. We saw youths being sent off into the woods to collect the people working or hunting there to come and look at us. We had again entered another era. Nearby, there had been a primitive village, which appeared on a British Museum map of the 12th century. The village had long since disappeared.

We held a Eucharist service and included everyone who had ever dwelt there, wondering what they had known about God. They may have heard travelling monks who would have preached to them or conducted a service in Latin but they would not have understood anything in Latin! So, in our service, aware of this situation we tried to release them by showing that it was possible for them to move on and start the journey towards Heaven. This extended our area of responsibility to include, as St Paul says, 'All men' to whom we proclaim and show forth.

# Bermuda Triangle

My wife and I were passengers on a small cargo ship bound for Jamaica. It was January and we were hardly out into the Atlantic before the storm hit us. To try and avoid the worst of it, the ship steered south and after a few rough days we found ourselves in the Sargasso sea, ploughing our way through islands of seaweed in between which were shoals of flying fish – a wonderful sight. Less wonderful were the plastic cups and bottles trapped in the weed. This seemed strange when there was no sight of any other shipping in the area.

Here the sea was somewhat calmer but one of the ship's boilers chose this moment to burst spraying us with water from the funnel as we sat on deck for the first time and delaying us for two days more. As we drifted gently in the now warm and steamy atmosphere, I became aware of a continuous sound like mournful singing. It was particularly clear when we were in our cabin. I thought it must be a record player in the crew's quarters and as it continued through a second night, I finally, in exasperation, went below to ask if it could be stopped. However, the sound down there was the same as it was everywhere else and the crew were equally mystified.

On the third day the engines were restarted and we slowly made our way to Kingston. The incident was forgotten until, on my return home, I started to read about the Bermuda Triangle and the history of that area. By chance I found a law book on the lawsuits of insurance companies against British sea captains of the 18th century who had been found to have thrown all their slaves overboard in order to make better speed. They received more money from the insurance claim than from selling the slaves in the cotton-fields. It was an extraordinary and cruel trade.

I discussed the subject some time later when I was speaking at a monastery in Yorkshire and one of the senior monks suggested that we should raise the matter at Mass the following morning when we could apologise to God for what our ancestors had done in the past. This we did and following the service three bishops in the north of England ordered the publication of the events to encourage other churches to pray in the same way; and to pray for those who had died so cruelly that they might forgive, and to ask that the path to Heaven might be shown to them. The date was June 1977 so the service was referred to as the Jubilee Eucharist.

The area known as the Bermuda Triangle had long been

known for the many mysteries surrounding the unexplained disappearances of ships and aeroplanes in the region. A few weeks after the service, an American newspaper contacted me enquiring what had made these incidents suddenly come to a halt. Six months later there had still been no further unexplained disasters and at the end of the year, the Bishop of Bermuda proposed a similar service to be held in his cathedral and another clergyman, Father Don Oman, suggested that one should also be held out at sea.

The Bishop set up a scientific team to monitor the accidents while I contacted the Florida coastguard who informed me that up to that time an average of one ship a month and one aeroplane every thirteen months had been lost without trace. The last one to vanish was a large Japanese cargo vessel in apparently calm weather. Two years after the service had been held, *The National Enquirer*, a popular American paper, asked my permission to write up the story of what we had done. Ten and a half years later the Australian Broadcasting Company researched through their library for a programme and found that there had been no more unexplained disasters within the Bermuda Triangle.

The Triangle is known to be an area of sudden squalls and cyclonic storms. Captains of ships and planes have reported before going missing that they were being spun round, that their compasses had failed and they had lost their bearings. However, if all these disasters could be explained by natural causes, why should a Eucharist service apparently bring it all to an end? Surely it must be that those people who had no one to appeal to for help and who had weighed down the ships and aeroplanes that crossed the spot where they died, had at last been released.

# The Diary

A family moved into a large house in a Forest in the south of England. It had once been the home of a well-known writer who, in his later days had been a great believer in Spiritualism and had held weekly seances there. He had long since died but this family discovered that many of the locals were convinced the house was haunted and did their best to avoid going near it. Even one of the postmen was afraid to walk up the drive.

The family, however, was not inclined to worry about ghosts and settled in happily. But it was not long before the father began to hear odd noises round the house for which he could find no explanation. Then, at Christmas, the eldest girl in the family, in her late teens and healthily sceptical about such things, came to stay for a few days. Normally a sound sleeper, she woke in the middle of the night imagining she heard someone moving around in the attic above. Having heard the stories about the house she began to feel frightened. Knowing it was possible to talk to God in her mind she felt that, if this was the writer trying to communicate, then perhaps she could do the same with him, so she said to herself, 'Please, Mr . . ., if it is you, please let me know what you want and then leave us alone and please don't frighten my brothers.' A picture came into her mind of a very kind face and she felt he was saying, 'Don't be afraid. I'm looking for a red leather diary. My wife wants me to write my memoirs. If you ever find it please leave it outside the front door. I won't disturb you again. I am so glad a family is now living in the house.' Immediately all fear left her. She felt a slight breeze pass through the room, after which she felt at peace and fell asleep.

Following this, the father visited the local vicar and told him of these happenings. The vicar apparently knew all about the various rumours surrounding the house and reported 'appearances' but had not known who it was who was 'appearing'. He asked that if the diary were ever found that it should be taken straight to him. 'I knew the man and what the red diary contained. We will burn it without anyone being allowed to read it, then I will come to your house and deal with the situation.' A few days later he did come and prayers were said in different parts of the house. The family and a few church friends joined in.

Not long after, a short article appeared in a daily newspaper reporting that a spiritualist medium had 'received' a message from this writer apologising for having misled people during his life! The house itself has remained at peace but the diary was never found.

A few days later a short article appeared in the *Daily Mail* saying that Madame Roberts, a famous medium in Kent, had at last received a message from this writer. Before he died he had promised that he would come back but had never done so and no one had ever 'met him' or heard anything from him, in spite of many attempts to arrange meetings. Now he was saying to the medium, 'I wish to apologise for having misled people during my life.' Extraordinarily – if he himself had been involved in spiritualist seances and investigation of witchcraft and similar subjects, and was now apologising for having misled people – then Madame Roberts was apologising for the very thing that she was actually doing, which seemed remarkably honest!

Within ten days of this there was an item in a newspaper about the old surgery in London where the writer used to work. The hall porter there said that for some strange reason the lift was out of control for a whole week. Whether it was supposed to go up or down, it always stopped opposite the surgery and the lift doors opened and then shut, and then it continued on its way. During this period three of the writer's relatives visited the house in the Forest where they had stayed as children. They asked what was happening because they had felt very peaceful recently. They were delighted when they heard the story; one of them clearly remembered seeing the red diary, although he had never been allowed to handle it and did not know what it contained.

The children of the house never heard or saw the old man again. The postman realised that he could go fearlessly up the drive to the house to deliver the mail. Other tradesmen followed suit and people began to walk past the entrance without any qualms. Indeed, some villagers even asked if they might visit the house because they had never set eyes on it, being too scared to go near it. In the twenty-five years since then, the place has remained absolutely peaceful.

# Chang

When I was in Peking, I became friendly with a young man who was keen to learn all he could about the Western way of life. I used to read with him and taught him to pray. He attended an engineering college where all the one storeyed buildings were built around courtyards. One night the students were awakened by a scream that there was a ghost outside. In Chinese fokelore this was an indication that somebody was going to die, so the boys were very frightened and hid underneath their iron beds. My young friend decided not to give in to this superstition so he knelt by his bed and started to pray. He felt strongly that he was being told not to be afraid and that he would be shown what to do. Then in the pitch darkness, he got up, crept along the dormitory and opened the door. Outside stood a white figure in the moonlight. The young man could not see a face and he crept up very, very slowly and stealthily and then jumped on the figure. To his amazement it was one of his fellow students who had wrapped himself in his sheet and gone out to watch the moon and the stars. He had not heard the commotion and was just sitting enjoying the beauty of the night. Of course, when the others came out to see what had happened, there was tremendous laughter and relief and my young friend was congratulated upon his courage.

But that was not the end of his story for his courage grew ever greater.

One day the Japanese army arrived at the college. After they had taken Peking, they usually broke in everywhere, beat people up or often even killed them. Then they would appoint a Japanese soldier to oversee each particular place. People were naturally very frightened. So when the Japanese troops came to the college, they smashed down the front gates and surrounded it. Those students who had not already escaped over the walls, hid. My new friend knelt down and prayed. He felt that the Lord was saying to him, 'These are your guests.' Entirely on his own, with no staff present, he went outside and bowed in front of the Japanese in welcome, offering to show them around. He took a group of them into the kitchens where they all sat down and had tea together. He was extremely polite and finally they departed, exchanging bows with him before they marched away. No one had been hurt. Once again the youth was regarded as a great hero. He was a wonderful person and later played a part in many of our adventures in Northern China.

# The Ranch

The valleys of California are full of ranches. Often, they are very small and overcrowded and their owners have raped the land bare of all greenery. It is the city dwellers dream to be able to escape to their 'ranch'. One such family bought five acres of land there and built a large house there. There were no trees on this land, just endless wooden fences, enclosing areas, and a few animals; horses, a donkey, sheep, several fierce dogs and geese. The family were sensitive and artistic and after moving in two of them developed urticaria (swollen, red, itchy skin). One developed breathlessness, palpitation and intense fear, while the father was aware of a constant smell of burning hair. One of the children was treated in hospital with corticosteroids which produced many unfortunate side-effects but did not alleviate his symptoms.

When the history of this place was investigated, it was found that in 1820, Red Indians had attacked a 'Mission Station' which had been located nearby. They were rebelling against the Spanish soldiers who had forced them to hard labour. The soldiers locked themselves in the church, knowing that the Red Indians respected God while the Indians locked themselves in the Spanish barracks. During the night the soldiers burned down the barracks. No apology, no service, no burial for these Indians had ever been carried out. One hundred and sixty five years later all that remained of this site was a heap of rubble.

An open-air, Requiem Mass was organised at the site and the new owners of the ranch apologised to the Red Indians of the neighbouring reserve. This was well received by the Indians and the news was passed to other reservations. Despite this, the family decided to return to the city where they were completely free from all their ailments. In their half an acre of garden they ensconced their animals from 'the ranch'. They, too, had suffered from strange ailments which the local vet had been unable to cure. They too all recovered.

Six months later all was not well. The family had put the ranch up for sale but there had been no buyers and every time they went there the sense of fear and feelings of breathlessness and the smell of burning returned and it took them about three days to recover their health after each visit.

We went to the ranch with an Episcopal priest. On the way, the car passed through mountainous country and the priest pointed out a cave in the mountainside saying, 'Stone Age men lived there; wall paintings and stone implements have been found from many thousands of years ago.' We asked what had ended their existence, he told us, 'It was the early ancestors of the Red Indians from the North.'

We decided to call on the Chief of the Schumach tribe and he and his wife came very willingly to our celebration at the ranch. The Chief was interested because his 'Grandfather', the very old retired chief, had decreed that it was time the tribe's prayer secrets were shared with the world. In the ranch house speaking on behalf of his tribe he apologised to God for having wiped out the Stone Age men; then the Spaniards present apologised for the killing and exploitation of the Red Indians in the 18th century and the Americans apologised for killing the Spaniards. The Indian prayer ritual was beautiful. Everyone sat on the floor, as one person prayed, and the Chief extended his left hand to everyone to receive the prayer, then cupped his right hand over it to add his own prayer. When the Bible was being read, he held up a hawk's wing in the air, indicating, 'We are hearing the truth'. At one point he laid two eagle's feathers in front of himself on the floor. Then he held them extended to all points of the compass and tapped them together in each direction. Later he burned some herbs making a blue smoke trail curling up to the ceiling. After the Eucharist we all made a full circle around the outside of the building, while the priest sprinkled holy water and everyone repeated the Lord's Prayer.

We drove to the site of the original burned-out Mission Station where the Red Indians had been killed and we offered more prayers. One of our group laid a bunch of Easter lilies there. This person had come from a neighbouring ranch becuuse of the break up of her own family nine years before. The next day unity in that family was restored. And the family who had suffered so many physical ill effects suffered none on this visit and three days later the ranch was successfully sold.

# The Conquerors

On the southern border of Texas, thirty miles from Mexico, out in the flat 'desert' is a prosperous 450 acre ranch where forty people live. Pumping water from the strata below has resulted in three lakes of about an acre each, fully stocked with catfish. Sixty cattle feed on lush pastures, while orchards and vineyards and young woodland have transformed the skyline. In the north western corner of the area, however, it is very bare and always feels cold. No one likes to work there. When we went to investigate, we had a feeling that men had died there. They could have been Spanish troops trying to use a shortcut in order to avoid the Indians, who lived along the river, or later explorers travelling towards the mountains of southern Arizona and California in the gold rush days. We did not know, so a Mass

43

of the Resurrection was held at the place for 'whoever' required it. Within a few days the whole of the little community felt that the area had been cleansed and set free and was now ready for working.

# The Boots in the Mud

In the pulpit of his village church a preacher, who had always been a kindly gentle person, began to suffer attacks of breathlessness which gradually increased both in frequency and severity. The attacks were peculiar in that they began very suddenly, making him gasp for air, then in a few moments faded and he was able to continue speaking until the end of the service when he always apologised to his flock. His congregation became used to this happening but he consulted his doctor. No abnormalities were found and none of the various pills he tried were of any help.

When he came to see me I learned that the attacks began just as he was either beginning a prayer, reading, or preaching the sermon. They had increased in frequency over a period of twelve years: he was then in his late thirties. We decided to look at his Family Tree. He was surprisingly reluctant to give any details and the real struggle to be honest came at the point of accounting for his father's life. The latter had been an alcoholic, who had disappeared when his son was only four years old. Twenty-one years later the police had told his mother that at last they had been able to identify his body. A young patrol policeman walking along the city dockside at low tide one Sunday morning, saw a pair of boots upside-down in the mud. He had pulled at them, whereupon legs emerged. With help, he had discovered the body of a man. 'Presumed drowned while drunk,' had been the verdict but no identification had been established. He had had a pauper's burial with no one to mourn. Now he had been identified.

I told him, 'Your father did not drown. He suffocated in the mud having fallen in head first. You have known about his death for twelve years and in the pulpit you have been in the most appropriate place possible to mourn him and, by proxy, confess his sins and commit him to God.'

The preacher reacted very angrily, 'I've never heard such rubbish in my life; that's not scriptural,' he said and left suddenly. I had encountered this attitude so often before and felt sorry for his narrow, rigid, blinkered outlook. Three months later he telephoned me to say that he had had to leave his church as his attacks of breathlessness were now almost continuous. He asked whether I had any suggestions. I sent him to see an Anglican vicar whom I knew lived near his village. This was rather humiliating for him as he did not have a very high opinion of the Church of England. However with the help and guidance of this vicar at a Eucharist service, he was able on his knees to confess, mourn, apologise for and commit his father to God. His healing was immediate and permanent.

# The Lamp

It was New Year's Eve and midnight mass was being celebrated in the parish church. Two teenage girls arrived rather late but were in time to join the end of the queue to the altar. The vicar was puzzled because they only came half-way down the church and then remained standing there even after everyone else had returned to their seats. When the service was over the vicar stood at the porch door in the dim light saying goodnight to the congregation. The girls were the last to leave and they were strangers and he asked then why they had not come to the altar and they told him that the lady in front of them did not go up either and had blocked their way. The vicar said that he hadn't seen this person. 'Oh,' they said, 'she was tall and wore a long dark cloak, the kind that nurses wear, and she had a box of some kind hanging from her hand.' He had heard a similar story before, and told them that Florence Nightingale was buried in the churchyard and her home had been nearby.

A week later I was told of this event and repeated it to another clergyman and his wife who were visiting me. The vicar's wife, a nurse, immediately told me, 'I've seen her too, she wanders St. Thomas's Hospital. Once when I was on night duty I saw her sitting by a medicine cabinet all night.' This has been confirmed by another nurse at St. Thomas's and yet another from one of its convalescent homes. We were puzzled. If the lady had been such an unselfish person, who had devoted her life in the Crimea to many thousands of wounded soldiers and had established the whole concept of nursing as a profession, why would she still be wandering the earth?

With a small group of friends, the vicar and I investigated the story of her personal life from the available literature and discovered that she had bitter battles with her mother and aunt. Her dedication and determination had enabled her to improve enormously the conditions and status of nurses but she had ridden roughshod over many other people's lives, including her own sister's.

We laid these facts before God on the altar at a Eucharist service, promising that we would continue to pray for her good intentions. Perhaps she is now free to go on her journey – certainly, she has not to my knowledge appeared again during the past four years.

# The Bypass

Britain's first dual carriageway was a most impressive sight and was opened by the then King. As the years went by it was regarded as being too narrow, too curved and quite inadequate. Increasing traffic often snarled the lanes and accidents became frequent. Local residents near one stretch lodged many complaints and the central road authorities had resurfaced and widened the road and added kerb stones and filters, removed bushes and erected metal barriers, but accidents continued.

One particular family had a strange experience, since when they have never ventured on this length of road. The husband and his wife were driving south, when suddenly they 'came to' or 'woke up'. He was lying in some bushes quite unharmed – his body somehow must have crossed the fast lane south, gone over the barrier, gone over the north-bound fast lane, then over both the slow lane and the grassy verge into the bushes. He walked to the nearest bridge and make his way back across the road to find his car in a ditch off the south-bound slow lane. His wife was missing. She was later found on the hillside above the car, also in some bushes and quite unharmed but very puzzled. When the car was pulled out they were amazed that it was in perfect condition without even a scratch. There seemed to be no rational explanation. Then one of their neighbours' told them that he had once been travelling south on his motorbike when, at the same stretch of road, he suddenly 'woke up' to find himself and his bike still pointing south but on another road – the old main road 500 yards to the west. Neither he nor his bike was damaged.

It was decided to study detailed maps of the area and

pin-point all the accidents. The chaplain of a nearby public school produced a very old map which we were able to enlarge and reproduce. Clearly marked on it, within one hundred yards of this site, were large circles identified as 'Plague Pits'. It is recorded that at the time of the plague in London in 1665, sufferers were ordered to stay in their houses, which were then boarded up. Many escaped by night and fled to other towns where the same thing happened. When all the occupants of a house were dead, carts would gather the corpses and tip them into large pits away from the town. Presumably, there was no mourning process or burial service for these people as the 'vapours or miasmas' were regarded at that time as very dangerous and no one would venture near them, if they could avoid it.

Early one morning, three Anglican priests, two Roman Catholic Jesuit priests, the school's headmaster and I met. Screened by some bushes at the edge of the pit nearest the road we set up a small altar, having asked others to join in prayer in their own homes at the same time. We were trying, as St. Paul commands, to 'show forth the Lord's death' and we held a Eucharistic service and preached.

Visual imagery on these occasions is very vivid. We seemed to see hundreds of lonely, bowed figures wandering in a dull twilight. Their appearance was utterly dejected; they looked at the ground as they walked. None sat or lay down; they were quite unaware of each other, seemingly walking through each other and through the traffic, quite oblivious of the vehicles. They were clothed in monotonous dark brown sacking and all appeared to be much the same size; there were no children. At this point, half way through our service, one of the figures came to the edge of the pit and fell on her knees, scratching at the turf and crying, 'Where's my baby?' over and over again. Then another woman came up behind her and touched her on the shoulder and said 'I'm your baby'. They hugged each other in joy and recognition.

An old bearded man came forward to the pit and cried out, 'Where's my daughter?' over and over again. And a woman came up to him and they too had a joyful reunion presumably not by physical but by spiritual recognition. Other people approached each other in the same way and as families were brought together they moved out of the twilight into a brighter light wearing whiter clothing where angels guided them away. We did not see everyone going away, but presumed that now the process had started, the remaining 'wanderers' would gradually begin their own journey.

Some five months later I recommended to a patient that we should hold a similar service for her ancestry. Her husband worked for the Ministry of Transport, investigating accidents and was very interested in this particular site. Over the years many safety systems had been tried on this road and recently the approach roads to the area had been resurfaced with alternately rough and smooth tarmacadam surfaces to slow drivers down. Her husband explained, 'The problem is that now there are no longer any accidents at this site we are not sure which alteration of ours has done the trick.' Immediately I pinpointed the date and time when they ceased. 'Yes', he said, 'that's just about the right time.'

We concluded that the lost souls whom we saw had no intention of causing accidents and were possibly not even aware of the disasters they produced. In their lost, wandering, unhappy state they were seeking any sensitive beings in order to attract attention. Although they could pass through road traffic, they momentarily distracted the drivers who were able to pick up their presence. The consequent momentary amnesia caused the accidents.

There are still accidents on this road, because it is narrow and mechanised fault and human error is always possible, but there have been no more recorded of this strange amnesic variety.

# Grandpa's Journey

The children as they grew up had always been used to their Grandpa standing at the foot of their beds when they awoke in the morning. He had died long before they were born but they recognised him from photographs. He was always crying and when they said, 'go away, we've got to get up', or 'we must get ready for school, don't bother us,' he would fade away. They were never frightened by him and their parents had never seen him.

When one of the girls was eighteen she became bulimic (the vomiting form of anorexia nervosa) which often indicates a psychosomatic reaction to a possibly unknown family secret. On exploring the Family Tree, such a secret was revealed. Her aunt had had an abortion before her marriage. At the Eucharist service to apologise for this, the girl saw a nineteen year old boy, whose name she knew, go down through a vast sheet of water and then emerge on the other side into a brighter light. Then she saw her Grandpa. He was standing on the other side of the water and went to meet the boy. He threw his arms around the boy as they turned together and set off – up and away into bright light. Others confirmed that they had seen this happen. Then we realised what Grandpa had been waiting for. He had known that his grandson was still earthbound but had not the means to release him. The teenage girl said that not only had her bulimia ended on that day, but a very strange symptom had also disappeared. She had never been able to put her feet into water – whether bowl, bath or sea – but had always used a wet cloth. Now she felt freed from this inhibition. Perhaps her cousin had been trying to tell her that he was prevented from crossing the River Jordan. He has never appeared again.

One year later the uncle and aunt admitted there had been an abortion twenty years earlier. They were then able to apologise to God, mourn and express their love for the child.

# The Court House

A long discarded tin mine in Cornwall was situated at the brow of a cliff. The low walls of the smelting sheds were still several feet high and the chimney was intact. Further along the cliff there were tracks leading down to the openings of ventilation shafts – very small openings enabling miners to get in and out near the galleries.

Halfway between the mine and the village and half a mile inland, was a long low building known as the Court House. It had been taken over by a group of young Americans who intended to turn it into a restaurant as tourists were beginning to come to the area. Their nights were extremely disturbed, by numerous human voices calling out and screaming. Although the house was situated on an exposed clifftop and the noise of the wind 'plays tricks' with the mind, they knew that this was not wind. They learned that the villagers always shut themselves in their houses at night, closing their curtains and not looking out for fear of seeing bloody bodies and hearing screams.

The Americans asked for our help. We sought the bishop's permission to hold a service at the site but he sent us to the rural dean, who, in turn, said it was the province of the parish priest. The latter considered the idea nonsensical but if we insisted asked that we would tell him which day we were coming so that he could absent himself. On the night prior to our arrival in the village, we stayed at a nearby town. During the night I awakened suddenly and heard the words,

'You are to preach to the departed'. I was not sure what was meant but when we reached the village the next day we decided to do as we were bid. Several clergymen dressed in ordinary clothes, joined us, together with some students and evangelical Roman Catholics.

It was a blustery, dull and wet day but the walls of the old smelting sheds gave us some shelter as we settled down on the tufted grass and sang to the accompaniment of guitars. First we had a period of 'free prayer' (that's when anyone can announce their intentions) followed by an account, in the form of a long story, of the life of Jesus Christ and His work accomplished on the cross. With the wind whistling above us we became aware that a crowd of beings was watching us and listening. There were many questions in our minds as we tried to mourn the dead and commit them to God. After two hours we moved to the village church, which had been left open, although the vicar himself was absent. We sang hymns and read from the bible at the lectern. By now, hungry and cold, we went out to buy food and asked the villagers about the old mine. Apparently, there had been a disaster in the 1860's. The sea had broken into the tunnels and over a hundred miners had been drowned. There were no graves in existence and no funeral service had been held for the drowned miners. When the villagers told us what happened at night, we eventually realised that they were describing children – MINORS – who, indeed, in those days had been the MINERS. The owners would collect waifs and strays from the cities, especially in the Midlands, and lure them to the mines with the promise of food and shelter. The advantages to the mine owners were that the children did not cost much to keep; they could huddle together to sleep taking up little space and they did not eat as much food as men. Being small the children could creep into the narrowest galleries for the ore, far less work to construct than those needed for a man's size.

If they fell ill and died no one knew or cared, for there were no families to answer to.

When over a hundred people, mostly children, were drowned, there was much gossip. But there was no way to recover the bodies and no relatives to mourn them or question their loss.

The callousness of the slave trade had been dealt with officially by Parliament but had not yet penetrated as far as life in the Cornish tin mines. As we continue to remember the children of that particular village, the 'unreleased' minors of other villages on those bleak hills will also find the escape road to the Kingdom.

# The Roman Soldier

As we traced the Family Tree of an old and noble family back to the twelfth century, we found enough evidence of wrongdoing, and torturing; (torture chambers, dungeons, evil practices of all kinds), for a full Requiem Mass. A Roman Catholic priest agreed to help us and offered the use of his church. We accepted his offer and the doors were locked. In addition to the Requiem, the lady representing the family, was to read out the long list of wrongdoings to be confessed.

In the middle of her reading, suddenly she stopped and said 'May I include the Roman soldier?' We gave her permission and she prayed for a Roman soldier and then continued with her reading. After the service I enquired who this soldier was thinking that somehow she had switched into an earlier generation. 'Didn't you see him?' she replied. 'He appeared standing just there, short and dusty with dark curly hair, wearing a metalled vest and skirt and leather sandals. He was so pleased to be included.' Then

53

when I told the priest this, he threw up his hands in despair, muttering, 'this is terrible'.

'Surely, it's good he has been released too,' I said.

'Yes, that's good,' said the priest, 'but think of the hundreds of Requiems I've held here, the thousands of names I have read out – with what result? None that I know of but now everything has changed. This is the first time in my church that a family has been present and prayed aloud their own intentions. At last, the soldier was included; he has been waiting here for 1800 years. Do you know that we are standing at this moment right beside a Roman road – he must have died here. Perhaps he was the leader of a cohort and represented them all. Now he can go free.'

# The Chappati Box

While I was speaking at a conference in India, I mentioned that our sub-conscious could pick up an awareness of lost souls. Afterwards, two young Hindu sisters aged twenty-four and eighteen came to tell me about their experiences.

Throughout their childhood, they had become used to children's voices calling out during the silence of the night 'Mother help me'. Every morning when they went into the kitchen, the water jar and the chappati box (containing thin discs of baked dough used as bread) were in the middle of the floor. They said that their mother was a very angry woman. She was especially angry with God since, just after her second daughter was born, she became pregnant again and produced twin boys who were born dead. Without ceremony she had dug a hole at the bottom of their yard, put the twin boys in a cardboard box and buried them herself.

I explained to the girls that the Hindu prophets had

foretold the pattern of the coming Christ hundreds of years ago and they very willingly took it upon themselves to give names to their brothers and commit them to God, accepting that the only way to God was through Jesus Christ.

Great peace came to the girls and their mother told them that the chappati box never moved again.

# The Jumbo

Bombay is a very disturbed city; every strata of its materialistic society is dependent upon another, from the wealthy penthouse dwellers at the top of their own skyscrapers to the beggars' birthplace and home amid the noise and stench of the streets. Their 'home' is just a few feet of the pavement, at night only.

The Air India Jumbo aeroplane disaster in which 380 people died when it plummeted into the sea immediately after take-off, caused a wave of unexpected visitations throughout the city. Most of the crew were Bombay people with their homes and relatives and friends in the city. Some off duty stewardesses were aware of their dead comrades visiting them. Their death had been so sudden, so absolute; they were mostly young, few of them were prepared for any other life. A highly paid élite who had seen the world – small wonder that the shock of eternity was very great to them.

We were able to pray with their living comrades and we raised the theme of forgiveness and deliverance in several churches of different denominations in Bombay. Many of them were grateful and still keep in touch with me.

# Air Disaster

Concussion, followed by amnesia combined with the self preservation instinct had totally confused my patient. He had been Island hopping in a light plane with some friends but the pilot had mistaken the signals from the ground, missed a landing, bounced off a rock and crashed the plane into the sea. Eight of the ten people aboard had died and their bodies were never recovered. Angry relatives tried to bring law suits but the owners stalled for years. My patient was dragged from the sea and because he was a key witness he was constantly badgered by lawyers and even government departments.

His parents had always drilled into him that his birth was 'an unwelcome mistake' and they had aborted several other pregnancies. After the accident he developed migraines and crippling pains on the left side of his body in the arm, chest and leg. X-rays and physical tests reveled no damage: drug therapy was begun finally leading to the administration of large dosages of an addictive drug, a close imitation of morphia. He made several suicidal attempts followed by admission to various mental hospitals. Psychotropic drugs, anti-depressants and tranquillisers were all tried to no avail.

Everything having failed, his G.P. consulted me. I interpreted the left-sided pains as psychosomatic – and suggested that we should look at the symptoms of depression, sleep disturbance and headaches objectively. No one had given any thought to the situation of those who had died in the plane crash some of whom obviously needed forgiveness and all of whom needed to be mourned and committed to God. With the help of the patient's wife we mourned them and committed them to God. The following year saw the happy birth of their first child. Life began anew for them with a different house, new neighbours and church. My task successfully completed I stepped out of their lives, a painful reminder of unhappy times.

# The Little Ghost

Everyone in the village knew that the house was haunted; even visitors had seen the small boy, somtimes in the middle of the night. The local vicar had been called in to perform an exorcism during which a shadowy figure had shot past the assembled company and out of the front door. People congratulated the vicar on the miracle. However, the next day the boy appeared in his parents' bedroom. I was asked to visit them and to stay overnight. As is my custom, we drew up the Family Tree and found that, as well as three perfectly fit teenagers, there had been a fourth baby, a boy, who was born dead about eleven years previously. 'Thank goodness', said the mother, 'I didn't want any more children.'

On the next night the figure again appeared in his parents' bedroom. This time the mother said aloud, 'If you are my little son, welcome into the family.' He went over to them and sat on the bed – they both saw the sagging of the bedclothes, and burst into floods of tears. Their immediate reaction was to go to the vicar and ask him to conduct a service. During the service the little boy came into the church. He was smiling and lively and in our visual imagery we saw him run over to where Jesus Christ was standing who took him into His arms.

At home, his parents told their other children about the boy and they were very excited to learn that they had a younger brother. The whole village delighted in this new experience. The local prostitute showed the most marked change – she joined the church and put right many of the things that she had done wrong, including apologising for her abortions.

Ghosts are not necessarily evil. They may have committed mis-deeds in life and therefore have been used by Satan. Exorcism is the means of getting rid of Satan and his servants. After working in this field for thirty years – and in the early days I had tried to exorcise everything – I am now convinced that Satan may be present in all situations. But an actual church service of exorcism is only necessary in about one per cent of the cases that are brought to me. The Lord's Prayer has an adequate exorcism in the last line if it is used specifically for that purpose.

# The Abbey

The new Canon was passing along the west wing of the abbey with his assistant. He noticed that this west wing was strangely empty and cold. It was the only area in the abbey without any furnishings, a forty-five foot square of stone flagging. He also noticed that in the aisles of the main chancel, near this area, up against the massive pillars, there was a smell of incense. His assistant said that he would search the records to see what had happened there.

He discovered that in earlier times a castle with a Norman tower situated on a hilltop guarded the port below. Knights lived there and ruled the countryside, taking whatever they wanted for themselves. There was much cruelty, frequent killings and the local peasants looked to the abbey for their protection. The abbey had been built by the Normans; it was a massive stone building, replacing the

Saxon monastery of clay and wattle. Suffering great hardship, the peasants herded together and built their homes up against the abbey walls so that in this position they had some strength. Their own naturally selected leaders were unable to do much but a plot was hatched to gain their revenge on the knights.

A message reached the castle that all the peasants' leaders were going to a service in the abbey so the knights, thinking that this would be an opportunity to dispose of them, also went. At a given signal the peasants produced weapons they had secreted and a bloody battle ensued in the west wing. The monks, apparently, were absent and the knights were killed.

We decided to hold a service in the west wing because there were no records of any burials or any services for the dead being held and no records of any confessions of guilt being made. For the occasion, we set up the area as a chapel when all the visitors had left and the abbey had been locked up for the night. There were twelve of us present and during the ensuing service we were aware that a band of knights knelt at the altar and laid down their swords while the 'incense of our prayers' pervaded the atmosphere. The area in which this was strongest was where centuries before the poor peasants had been allowed to stand to listen to the services. (The gentry and knights occupied the central nave.) Perhaps the humble folk's prayers were the ones that had been heard in Heaven – strange, because the services in those days were conducted in Latin and they would have been the least able to understand the words. Finally, several of us went to the Norman tower, a sad little ruin mainly consisting of very thick walls. In the small room spaces we prayed and apologised for all the debauchery and murder that had been perpetrated there.

The west wing of the abbey is now furnished and retains a marked sense of peace and warmth.

# The Somme

After his father died, Arthur aged twenty-three was a changed man. He had been a sensitive, helpful youth particularly caring for the aged and infirm but now he became very disturbed. He heard voices, lay on the ground in public places and had gory dreams of butchers cutting up people. His father, Thomas, had been a gentle quiet man: a Quaker. In his sixties he had suddenly had a heart attack, without any warning symptoms, and died.

Arthur was treated by psychiatrists; had ECT and many drug trials. He had been a regular church goer with his mother and brother and, gradually, some stability was achieved although for some time he refused to communicate at the Eucharist service. His mother had prayed for all the wrongdoings of her own antecedents.

When Fred, her younger son, became twenty-three years old, he too began to show exactly the same symptoms as his brother – including hearing voices, gory dreams, lying on the ground and frontal headaches like sharp pains. He, too, was given heavy sedation and was treated by psychiatrists. The doctors contained the boys' disturbances but in no way cured them.

Their father, Thomas, was born in 1913 and named after his only Uncle Thomas who died three years later aged twenty-three in the trenches of the Somme in France. Neither his parents nor his brother were in any way prayerful people and Thomas, although he carried the same name and the responsibility would not have known how to pray for his soldier Uncle. Quakers do not celebrate Holy Communion – they believe that every meal should be a communion. Thus, when Uncle Thomas died all the responsibility for him fell upon Arthur when he reached the age at which the soldier had died. Their symptoms matched – from the head pains to the lying down in public and feeling terrified and wounded.

Arthur, not knowing the facts about Uncle Thomas' death, gradually emerged from the pressure, especially after his successful marriage. It seemed that Uncle Thomas therefore turned his attention to Fred when he reached the same age at which he had died. Now both sons are able to pray about it and an improvement in their condition began immediately. The process of weaning them away from all the drugs, however, was a long, slow and difficult road and took many months. But it was successfully achieved in the end.


# Bodenstown


Robert Cielou wrote a book in 1983 called, *Spare My Tortured People*, which is a history of the troubles in Northern Ireland. He told me that he had been unable to reach any conclusion in this book. But as we talked together we realised that the violence seemed to stem from many of the same families, generation after generation, and he pointed out that Sinn Fein followers, 'recognise no validity in the normal democratic process because . . . all legitimate authority is derived only from the generations of the dead who died for Ireland and is properly wielded in the present by the organisation of men and women prepared to repeat the

61

blood sacrifice.' He calls them 'aristocrats,' 'Samurai,' the 'military elite.' He quotes Dr. Cruise O'Brien as saying, 'this cult of the dead is such a preoccupation of the IRA and since they show such a complete disregard for the sanctity of life, it might be worthwhile examining this strange phenomenon.' They have, he says, an intense preoccupation with Bodenstown. This is a graveyard, for the Sinn Fein, a place 'set apart' which is a rallying ground for meetings on certain dates throughout the year. 'This,' as he goes on to say, 'is pure paganism.'

Men on both sides in Northern Ireland talk of revenge for their ancestors or for those more recently killed in the conflict so we are all embroiled as skeletons of the past fight skeletons of the past. Arms dealers, communists, occultists and other subversive forces all benefit from the disruption of Ulster's society. But, these people too are being used; the only common denominator would seem to be Satan who is manipulating everyone like puppets on strings. We know that Satan was defeated at the Cross. We must bear witness to this and repeat services for those for whom no confession has ever been heard so that they will no longer need to haunt their descendants.


# Northern Ireland


Neil Carlan is a very alert young priest who has a fellowship of about sixty ex-IRA men in the Maze Prison. Outside the prison he has an enormous following of Catholics involved with reconciliation. He called me there to help him to explain the need for a change of attitudes and the culmination of our meetings was a Mass held with the specific intention of praying for those who had died in violence. About one hundred and twenty people attended, many of whom were either ex-prisoners, or widows or wives of members of the IRA. Our intention was to release the dead so that they would not continue to possess the living. All was going well and many had drawn up their Family Trees and were praying aloud. Suddenly there was a very loud banging on the door and a woman burst in. The priest asked me to take her into another room and talk to her so that he could carry on with the service. She told me that her husband had been in prison as an IRA activist but had never returned home after completing his sentence two years ago. In the early hours of that morning, he had broken into their house, by smashing down the kitchen door, and had rushed upstairs to her bedroom shouting for help. Apparently he had been out on patrol when, in the darkness, his dead father suddenly appeared with his arms outstretched crying, 'Help, help.' The man was terrified, believing in the superstition that if you see a dead person you yourself are going to die. So he had fled from the patrol and had run home to his wife. After she had explained this to me, she joined in the service and was able to pray for her father-in-law. With a new sense of purpose and joy she returned home to reassure her husband that all would be well.

# The Castle Parapet

A family moved to a grey-stoned city house of the type that was part mews and part old courthouse, and they had the house blessed. Several years later, during redecoration, a trooper's sword was found. It was of the 1780 period and so positioned that it could easily have been drawn in an emergency. Soon afterwards, on three separate nights, the mother had been haunted by a leering male figure and a few days later both her sons admitted that they had seen him. Then her daughter telephoned from abroad to tell her mother about a terrifying experience that had happened to her.

During the night she had awakened to find a repulsive male figure stooping over her, jeering. Seeing him made her feel sick and she had a tremendous sense of fear. She could see him, despite the lack of light, whether her eyes were open or closed. He went out of the room, then returned, opening and closing the door on each occasion. His face was not clearly visible but he was wearing a long cloak. Fortunately the girl knew that she should repeat the Lord's Prayer and did so; and, as soon as she was able she telephoned her mother. Although she was so far away the family felt this incident must have been connected with the earlier history of their house, so they asked a priest to hold a Mass there.

A year later they moved to another city – but again the fearful apparition made itself felt. At this point I was asked to help. It was obvious to me that since this 'being' had followed them, he must be a family ancestor and not associated with a particular place. The mother had become aware of the Eucharistic approach to such problems so I concluded that the 'being' recognised that, through her, he had a chance of escape. He was not apparent all the time but 'visited' (in the words of the Old Testament 'The sins of the fathers are visited. . .').

We drew out the Family Tree and found that the family ramifications were endless. We traced back over a thousand names, many famous, but no startling evil was uncovered until the seventeenth century. Then a man, who had been an ordained Episcopal priest, had done nefarious deeds for

Charles I and then changed his allegiance when Cromwell was in power and signed false documents for him. He lived in a castle with a cellar full of gold and was able to save it from destruction by bribery. Only one other man lived in the castle with him; a tall, thin shadowy figure known as 'the murderer' who was only seen at night. (Later, in the reign of Charles II, the priest and this man should have been tried for practising witchcraft.) One night, during a thunderstorm the priest had gone out into the courtyard to deal with the dogs. A singularly bright flash of lightening struck a large stone section of the parapet; it broke loose and fell on him, crushing him. He was killed instantaneously. He had no known descendants though there were many other branches of the family.

We thought that the mother of this present-day family, knowing the priest's history, was in a position to help. We all went to a chapel to pray. While we were praying we became aware that the priest was there, in his cloak, but without his face or hands being visible. He was still living his last memories of misery, loneliness and terror. Then we saw some angels come and strip him of his long black cloak and he stood in a shaft of blinding light, unable to shield himself, naked and alone, the truth about him exposed.

The family promised to continue to pray for him at Mass and there has been no recurrence of the nightly visitations.


# The German Hospitals


The Channel Islands were occupied during the Second World War by the Germans who were preparing them as defensive outposts for the invasion of Britain.

About twenty-five years after the war ended, some youths complained that they heard 'voices'. Medical treatment from their doctors, who diagnosed them as schizophrenics, had not helped and they had no other symptoms apart from slight side effects from the drugs. I was consulted about them by two clergymen with whom I had worked previously. First, we set about learning all the details about the 'voices'. On the first day of 'hearing voices', the youths had been upstairs in the private room of an isolated cafe where they had been using a ouija board. The 'voices' they then heard continued with them even when they were back home, about six miles away. They did not understand the gutteral words of the 'voices' but were able to pronounce some of them like 'Ya'.

Six of us then decided to visit the cafe. It was an unexpected car ride out of the town along a five mile coastal strip dominated by tall cliffs. Along the coast road below the cliffs the land was sparse with no vegetation and until we were about half a mile from the mid-point, we saw no buildings. All along the sea side to the left of us was a continuous wall of concrete about thirty to forty feet high with irregular openings. The wall completely cut out the view of the sea. We then came to a low, sprawling, isolated building with a restaurant, bar and dance hall.

In the restaurant, we were taken upstairs to the small room where the youths had been when they first heard 'the voices' and which was used by the owners as an office. We sat round the table in the centre and had a long session of questions and answers. Apparently the Germans had built the concrete walling, which was a complex of gun emplacements and defence posts, against any invasion. At that time none of the Islanders were allowed into the whole five mile strip and both the approaches were fortified against intruders. This had involved a stupendous amount of labour so the Germans had brought over prisoners of war from Europe to do the work. They had come on the railways in closed cattle trucks and had been smuggled across the water at night to the Island, so that the prisoners did not know where they were and the Islanders did not observe them.

We were sitting in the room which had been the Headquarters of the SS. We remarked that from this room many people must have been sent to their deaths. 'Yes', said the residents, 'those concrete posts that you see are eight feet high; they used to be surrounded by barbed wire. Prisoners due to be punished were thrown there to die in full view of everyone; then they were thrown into concrete mixers; their fellow prisoners wrote their names with their fingers in the cement – there are hundreds of them. When the work was completed the Germans did not return the rest of the prisoners to camps but threw them all into the mixers so that no one could reveal the secrets of the defence emplacements. We reckon there are fifteen thousand bodies in this defence system alone.' This then explained the 'voices'; they were the anguished, murdered prisoners of war crying out.

We all gathered in a small church in the town to hold a service after which the youths were 'freed' from 'the voices'.

Some weeks later our attention was drawn to the existence of a vast underground network of halls and passages also built by prisoners of war for the Germans. These were to be fully equipped hospitals with wards ready for use during the invasion of England. They are now tourist places and visitors walk and drive through them. They are eerie, very cold and silent. A similar 'hospital' exists on Guernsey. The Roman Catholic priest on Guernsey went with several friends and colleagues, including two Jesuits and local Catholic doctors, down into the tunnels and prayed there at a Eucharistic service for the sins of the Nazis and for the murderer prisoners of war.

# B.B.C.

The young man was convinced that the voices from the B.B.C. were attacking him and that every television aerial on every house was screaming at him, to the effect that on Mussolini's order he was to be hung. This so disturbed him that he would bang on the windows and doors demanding that the aerials should be removed. Finally his family agreed that he must be certified and he was committed to a mental hospital. Medical attempts were made to control his delusions; he was diagnosed a schizophrenic and various drugs and treatments turned him into a bloated zombie-like human being. He was seldom fit enough to go home because of all the medication. Moreover his complaints against the B.B.C. (which only stopped when he was sedated at night) continued for a further eight years.

His parents were desperate. With his father, I began to explore the Family Tree but nothing seemed to be wrong: nobody unaccounted for; no disastrous deaths. I asked about war service. The family were Quakers, and therefore, conscientious objectors and had never been engaged in any war. Subsequently, the father returned to see me. He wondered whether it was of any significance that, 'over forty years ago my eldest sister, the boy's aunt, was engaged to an Italian. Just before the Second World War he was called up for military service and had to leave England. My sister and the whole family went to the ferry port with him to see him off across the Channel, for we loved him. From that day no one has heard of him again, not even his relations in Italy'.

Was he a 'conscientious objector who refused to carry a

gun and was court martialled and then hung.' I asked the father. His response was that he'd often wondered whether that was the way he had died. We decided to go to Holy Trinity Church, Brompton, to the regular service and there we prayed for the dead Italian. We had not told the son, who was in the mental hospital eighty miles away. Next morning the son telephoned his father to say that at last the B.B.C. voices had been switched off. When his aunt heard about this she started going to church. She had always loved her Italian fiance, but was happy with her husband and family. Then she had a dream. It began as a nightmare with the Italian being hung, then it was of the two of them swimming together in the beautiful warm sea and he was smiling at her.

It took eighteen months in a rehabilitation hospital to wean the patient from all the drugs and then the authorities said he was ready to go home. During that same weekend his aunt in her church had decided to say goodbye to the Italian she had known and loved.

# The Haunted Lookout

High on the cliff-top, a mile from a tiny Cornish village, was the look-out station, and below the cliffs, just under the surface of the heaving sea, the great rock which had spelt death to so many ships, some of them doubtless lured on to it by the local 'wreckers'. I had been asked to visit the spot because of unexplained noises during the night watch; sounds which penetrated even the howling wind and the rain squalls. My coastguard friend was frightened each time he had to take the 11 p.m. to 7 a.m. watch.

I searched along the cliff-top for any presence of evil. All seemed well apart from one promontory which felt extremely evil, cold and dark. This was clearly a place of human suffering. I returned to the flat area of the cliff in front of the look-out station and asked God for guidance in 'seeing' what had taken place. It appeared that many incidents had taken place there but the worst involved a sea-captain whom I visualised as a large, brutish man in a reefer jacket with a brass telescope under one arm. He was bellowing at his ragged crew who were struggling up the cliff with huge bundles of contraband goods. His bullying was doubtless due to fear of being caught by the authorities who constantly patrolled these cliffs. One of his exhausted crew stumbled and fell and in his fury, the captain lashed out at him verbally and physically and getting no response he then shot the poor fellow before turning back to urge the rest to greater effort.

As the shouts of the men and the wind died away in my head, I glanced towards the look-out where my friend was on duty. The afternoon was calm and sunny so I decided then and there to hold a service for the men I had seen. I had a friend with me and together we brought bread and wine from the car and placed it on the flat area near the look-out. As we said the Lord's Prayer together we were conscious of many more sailors of different nationalities gathering round; they were probably those who had died in shipwrecks on the rocks below. And as we ourselves took the bread and the wine, we made it clear that we were doing it on their behalf and we witnessed to our Lord Jesus Christ's achievements for us all. Gradually, it seemed, they began to rejoice with their hands held up high in thanks to God. We then asked God to send His angels to show them the way He had prepared for them to go.

When all was peaceful again, we took the remaining bread and wine to the look-out station. The coastguard greeted us and said, 'I forgot to tell you about the ghost in here. He is very friendly and just follows us about all the time. When I saw you lift up the bread and wine in the service, he said to me, 'Hey, don't forget me!'

Some time later the coastguard reported to me that there had been no more 'hauntings' and that the night watch now passed peacefully.

# The Season of Rebirth

It was spring time and the lambing 'season' occupied all hours of the day and night. Bales of straw gave shelter to the newly born lambs. I was staying on a hillside farm, dominated by a large and rambling, early Victorian, whitewashed house. I was a guest of the farmer's family, whom I had known for a year and was assigned to the master bedroom. It was very spacious with several radiators, a vast double bed and its own bathroom. It was a pleasure to be taken care of so well and even to be served with silver tableware! I planned to stay there for six days as it was a convenient centre for my lecture tour and for interviewing nearby patients.

On my first night, I was tired and fell asleep at once. At 3.55 a.m. I was awakened suddenly by a very large black heap sitting on my chest; my alarm was such that I could not breathe because it was so heavy. I struggled to repeat the Lord's Prayer but kept getting stuck. After pushing hard and then attempting to pray aloud, I eventually reached the last line, 'but deliver us from the evil one' and slowly, slowly I regained my normal breathing and then finally fell asleep.

At breakfast I mentioned the incident to my host. The fact that I had never before felt such oppression or anxiety

71

surprised my host who thought I would have experienced it on many occasions. Then he explained that he had deliberately not told me that the bedroom was haunted. Only three years earlier a lady occupying the room had been so distressed that she had hanged herself. And one of her sons, who slept in the next bedroom said he hated the master bedroom, and that he, too, had been awakened at 3.55 a.m. Apparently he had regular somnambulistic attacks during which he pulled over furniture, and smashed things around the house which then always awakened the other members of the family. For years the doctors had diagnosed epilepsy and just given him tablets. His attacks occurred only at night and the remainder of his sleeping hours were always extremely restless.

His Family Tree produced no disasters to account for this behaviour so I switched my search to discovering who had been the earlier inhabitants of the farmhouse. The old nanny of the previous family told us that the farmer and his wife had both died from natural causes and had left two sons. They had grown up there with the servants to look after them. The younger son was brain-damaged at birth and could only make gutteral sounds. When he reached puberty, he began to have epileptic-like seizures which later developed into major fits. At twenty-one he died, supposedly of pneumonia, and shortly after his death, his elder brother shot himself.

The room in which I was sleeping had been the elder brother's bedroom and the younger brother had occupied the room in which the surviving son, who had also developed epileptoid fits, now slept. My theory was that the elder son, desperate about his brain-damaged brother's constant interruption of life and total lack of communication, thought he would be better dead. Had he, perhaps, suffocated his brother as he slept, possibly around 3.55 a.m. and then, unable to carry the guilty secret, shot himself. If this was what had happened, then the Eucharist of the Resurrection would be appropriate, during which we could make a proxy confession and commital even though none of us present was related to the previous inhabitants. My hosts family together with three others joined in the simple service which we held in their drawing-room.

My remaining nights there, in the master bedroom, were completely undisturbed. However, because we hold one service we cannot always assume that a 'cure' is immediately complete. Those for whom we pray are able, it seems, to begin a journey, but on this journey there may be many stages and many wrongs they still have to face. In this case, since the first service, priests have visited the house several times and held a service in the master bedroom and sprinkled it with holy water. The son has still had the occasional fit over the succeeding years. But here lies his challenge. The 'epileptic' himself must come to terms with the process of his own spiritual development in this life.


# The Black Spot


Visiting Ireland and being made aware of the eternal world is a tremendous adventure: so much is represented there from the early Celts to the monastic era and to the present day destruction: vendettas, killings and famines. The Irish are a wonderful, warm, humerous and open people. They are very willing to begin a new chapter in their life but the old domination of the priests, who dealt with the illiterate peasants with Latin verses and candles, has left them'with a superstitious view of religion.

A Roman Catholic priest, who was very much accepted as

one of the community felt he had had to break through a legacy of mistrust. His predecessor had apparently buried his girl friend in the priest's plot. When he himself died, the gravediggers were not sure whether to bury him face up or down. Since then, there have been tales of previously buried priests being seen at night carrying their coffins up the road to the public cemetery.

On a nearby road there was an accident black spot where many strange disasters and deaths had happened; and just over an adjoining wall was a canal where suicides had drowned and a man had been hung from a tree. An ancient battle site lay within half a mile, on the edge of which lived a 'paranoid schizophrenic' who heard voices after a drunk neighbour committed suicide. Medical therapy was unable to help him. Some children in the area had seen 'ghosts' of other children in their bedrooms; and there was evidence of a rath or fairy ring. This is usually a circle of trees on a hilltop, within which a sunken area is used for burials – especially of children, including aborted babies – when a ceremony carried out by a priest is considered expensive and unnecessary. Mostly such raths are ancient and sacred, the one near the 'black spot' being just beside the children's home. The farmer, who owned the land had cut down all the trees, filled in the central pit and incorporated the area into his fields. After this happened the children began seeing the 'ghosts'. Also near the road, was a small disused graveyard in which unusual iron crosses stood among the many fallen gravestones. And there were many potholes where it was said children were buried.

The priest held a Mass of the Resurrection in a nearby house and each person present took a specific subject to pray about: a mother prayed for babies, a father for suicides; another one for careless drivers; another for farmers and another for battle sites. An Englishman apologised for past cruelties committed there. (There had once been a Cistercian monastery nearby and Cromwell's men had killed all the monks, executed the Abbot on his own altar and then gutted the building.) A business man apologised for the selfish exploitation of the land; and finally some children volunteered to pray for forgiveness for having played hide-and-seek in the cemetery and for covering the gravestones with graffiti.

At Christmas that year I received a card from a man who had attended the service. He wrote, 'You do not know me nor the fact that I was an epileptic, but I want to express my gratitude as I have not had a fit for the nine months following that service.'

# Blood Sugar

Physicians are accustomed to diagnosing, prescribing and neatly pigeon-holing a patients illness. Sometimes their methods are *too* neat and tidy.

Recently, a fifty year old patient told me that her diabetes had begun when her father died. I pricked up my ears at this. 'Why?' I asked. 'Oh,' she replied, 'he was a diabetic and died of gangrene.'

It then emerged that this man's own father, his grandfather's three brothers and his great grandmother had all died in the same way. Together the patient and I mapped out her grandmother's life. As an infant she lived in Brunswick in Germany. But when she was eight years old her parents told her that because there were too many children in the family, they were sending her to New York where she must find the orphan train; and then she would be adopted by a farmer in west America. The child was put on a stagecoach and had to make her way to the boat; arriving in New York she found the orphan train and, eventually, she was adopted by a farmer in the west of America. She was still only eight. I realised what had happened. Being abandoned was like a punch in the stomach for her; she could neither cry, nor eat, nor even be sick on the boat. The area of this 'psychological punch' is the pit of the stomach, behind which lies the pancreas where insulin is made. As this part of her body was virtually paralysed, her insulin production was diminished and her blood sugar level increased. This illness is diabetes. The great-grandmother died young but left four sons; so, generation after generation, the same 'disease' was passed on. My patient's daughter was a hospital laboratory technician who monitored her mother's blood sugar and found it to be running abnormally high.

My patient was a devout Roman Catholic and the Church told her that she was being haunted and possessed by her ancestors. They visited her because they trusted her and were trying to draw her attention to the area of 'unfinished business'. Thereafter she attended every Mass with the intention of confessing the cruelty of her great-great-grandparents and the resentment and anger of succeeding generations. Many times she told me she was aware of a vast circular pool of light in the church where the Lord would stoop down and lift someone out of it. At home she searched old photograph albums, in which she was able to recognise the released ancestor. Over a period of eight months she experienced this repeatedly and at each stage her blood sugar dropped. Finally, the last person to be lifted up by the Lord was her father, and then her blood sugar became normal. It has remained so and she keeps to a sensible diet and lives peacefully.

I have subsequently used this approach to diabetes successfully in many cases: ten were cured in this way in one year alone.

# Intensive Care

The neurological unit of one of our large hospitals had a young girl in intensive care who had been unconscious for ten days. She had been found in this state, rushed into the hospital and all the usual tests undertaken without results; tests for polio and other acute encephalitic (inflammation of the brain) reactions from early Rabies to Wernike's Encephalopathy (acute vitamin deficiency). I was asked to meet the parents and concerned friends. Another aspect of this girl's story was that her fiance had been killed in a car crash, and she in her grief had been trying to 'get in touch' with him. We had to put on gowns, cap and masks and gloves to visit her. This made it difficult for her to recognise anyone. However, I was determined to pray with her, and apologised to God that she had disobeyed His laws by trying to 'get in touch' with the dead. Up to this point she did not react. Nor did I expect any reaction for she had tubes up her nose and through her mouth; she was supposedly unconscious. But she started to cry and was obviously very much awake. We carried on a series of questions and answers as she was able to waggle her right toes for 'yes', her left for 'no'. When we left I told the nurse she could remove all the tubes and monitors. After that she was kept in the ordinary ward for a few days.

Later we instituted the Eucharist specifically for the committal of her fiance. At one of these Eucharists three people were sure they saw a blonde girl of twenty-four. We gave her a name and committed her to God. Her grandmother had been regarded as a 'fluctuating schizophrenic', and when questioned about her pregnancies admitted that she had had an abortion. Now she was told of this twenty-four year old and she connected this to her own child. The grandmother has shown no schizophrenic symptoms since then.

# Seven Thousand Miles

Beliefs and attitudes come to us through training, experience or revelation. In medicine the questing spirit of our training places us in an international, cooperative fraternity. This is not so with many theologians; some are so literally-minded and narrow that they will even kill to uphold their very particular interpretation of God's law. We saw this in the Iran–Iraq war. We were guilty of it in the days of the Spanish Inquisition.

I encountered it personally at a meeting I attended, with several hundred people present, where I was shouted down for quoting one helpful explanation by Professor William Barclay, because in one of his many books he has discussed the doctrine of Universalism. The man in the audience, who shouted at me, insisted that all *my* works should also be dismissed.

I encountered it again when a clergyman and his wife came to see me because their daughter in a far off country was extremely ill with anorexia. They wanted to know what they were to do? When we eventually came to drawing out names in their Family Tree, I asked about the unborn. There had been miscarriages, one before and one after the birth of the anorexic daughter. I suggested that these aborties shold be prayed for. This immediately raised an angry response from them.

'You may not pray for the dead', they said. To which I answered, 'God is a God of Love, I will talk to Him about anything I choose; nowhere in the Bible are we forbidden to talk to Him about the dead and in the Bible, Peter, Paul, Our Lord, Daniel, Aaraon, Elijah all did – so why not?' The clergyman's wife was the first to give her agreement; and so we held a service, and she was thrilled to see, in her visual imagery, two beautiful looking, fully-grown girls and hear their names. A few days later the wife received an airmail letter from her daughter saying, 'This afternoon I saw what a stupid life I have been living . . . all the fuss about food. I am going to be a normal person.'

The hour of her writing was *the same time as the service* – and yet she had not been informed at all of the event.

Similar curative experiences have happened in over eighty per cent of all the hundred and fifty anorexic and bulimic patients for whom I have been responsible for healing.


# The Distorted Buddhas

It was a very modern, semi-detached, house with a large front lawn and a beautifully landscaped garden. I had been called in to give a second opinion about a very small six year old who had a fever and epilepsy. On arrival at the house my immediate reaction was one of cold revulsion: for in the front garden in the bushes, on the path, in the vestibule, in the hall and in every room were Buddhist statues. Most were two to four feet high and made of cement or porcelain; some were rather gaudy; some terrifying; some contemplative. None were antiques or of any value. They were the type that can be obtained in garden centres or pseudo 'antique' shops.

My first question to the owner was 'Why?' 'Oh I like them, I collect them', was the owner's reply. But they are all distortions of the Buddha and his teaching', I told him.

When I was introduced to the little boy, he was fast asleep on a sofa. He had a high fever and a temperature of over 102°. I was told that he had had over a hundred 'convulsions' that day, and this was 'normal'. He was epileptic. Extensive medical tests and therapy had been unable to reach a conclusion about the cause of his condition.

I found that his reflexes were normal and there was no neck rigidity as one would find with meningeal irritation. His mother had always nursed him. She told me that he had a negative attitude and always said 'No' whatever the subject, whether food, play, travel. The seizures frequently caused him to fall down but without doing any damage to himself; mostly they appeared as *petit mal* and momentary 'absences'.

We drew up the Family Tree and found that a miscarriage in the past had been unmourned. We prayed about this and promised that the family would go to Mass and name the baby who miscarried. Then we laid our hands on the boy's hot little forehead and asked that the Lord's will be done. We did this in the late evening. In addition, his mother collected together all the Buddhist statues – there were at least thirty – and took them into the back yard and smashed them to powder with a sledge hammer.

The next day, and for the whole of the next week, the boy behaved as a normal happy child. He didn't have any 'fits' at all and his fever disappeared. And he lost his negative attitude. Subsequently I understand he has very rarely had a fit.

# I Thirst

The vicar had a problem. He was drinking nearly fifteen pints of alcohol a day. It mattered little to him what he drank but his alcoholic intake was so uncontrollable that he was about to be confined to an alcoholics institution. While talking to his wife, she admitted that they had had an abortion years earlier when they were both students. A friendly priest helped them to celebrate the Eucharist and to consecrate the unborn child in the service.

Early in the morning after the service, the vicar still half asleep thought he saw a burglar in his bedroom and struggled to wake up to confront him. The figure turned round and said; 'Daddy, my name is Ruth. I'm sixteen years old. All the other girls at school talk about their boyfriends and getting engaged, but in my world the males are so horrid, I don't want to have anything to do with them.' By then the vicar had got up and was walking towards the female figure. But when he stretched out his arms towards her she vanished. The shock of this vision made him lie down again. He thought about the words he had just heard. Suddenly, he realised that his wife's abortion had happened sixteen years earlier. A girl named Ruth was part of their family and was now on her way to heaven. He realised that it was Ruth who, for years, had been saying, 'I thirst, I thirst,' and that however much he drank or however frequently he drank, it had never slaked his thirst.

The vicar now no longer felt the need to drink. His alcoholic habit was broken.

# Cool My Tongue

A man, who for years had been involved in the care and healing of others and had drawn out many Family Trees and had seen many miracles, was challenged as to whether he had ever looked into his own Family Tree. At first, he said it was quite unnecessary as he knew all about his relatives. But he was then persuaded to draw out his Family Tree on paper and to account for everyone. In doing so, as a matter of little concern, he commented, 'Mother had a miscarriage between me and my brother.'

We held a service for this unborn baby and he heard later from his brother, who lived seven thousand miles away, that suddenly one day he had felt himself completely cured of his alcoholism. It was the same day as our service.

Perhaps this meant that the younger brother throughout the years had been hearing, 'I thirst,' as an unknown and unrecognised pressure on his subconscious, and the only way to lessen the pressure was by dulling the supra-conscious areas with alcohol. As in the Bible story of Dives and Lazarus, when the rich man Dives in his place of torment cried, 'Send Lazarus to me that he may dip the tip of his finger in water and cool my tongue.'

# Syracuse

The social problems of a certain area near Syracuse in New York State were very marked – murders, suicides and abortions – and the Franciscan priest in charge of the area wanted to know if we could solve some of their problems.

One of the first, and outstanding, problems was that the land there was part of an Indian reservation and that people were building holiday homes there without any permits and these homes were then becoming permanent residences. The Indian chiefs, who wanted to take this up with the American Government were always being fobbed off with the excuse, 'One day there will have to be a High Court case'. But over the years nothing was ever done.

To take in the atmosphere of the area we decided to drive there and on the roads we encountered various problem areas. One was of a battle site, where the English and French had paid Red Indians to fight against each other thus fragmenting the Mohawk tribe. The land was very marshy and in the area which had been chosen as the graveyard for the battle dead they had been unable to dig down very far; and over many years, skeletons had come to the surface. Consequently people didn't like living near the area. We also found that there were places known as safe houses. These were houses with a third storey from whose windows people could monitor the movement of Government forces. These houses were also used for what was known as the underground railway; a smuggling system for getting slaves into Canada from the South.

Suddenly, as we were driving along a main road, three cars in front of us collided at a crossing. We stopped and found that just a hundred yards ahead of the cars a light plane had just crashed and that the cars had hit each other in avoiding the plane. We then turned north off the main road onto a side road and came to a lake. At the lakeside, we were surprised to find police cars and frogmen because just a few hours earlier a fishing boat had sunk with all on board.

Our next stop was at a friend's house; here we were to have a meal and discuss the family problems – the husband had just announced that he was buying a flat in the city near his work and was leaving the family home to live there.

Later that same evening we were ready to say a Mass for all these troubled occurrences. The six year old daughter of the family, who should have been in bed long ago, curled up on the sofa beside her father and fell asleep during our service. Different members said appropriate prayers of apology to God for all the things we had recently witnessed and been involved with. At the end of the service the daughter was woken up and told to go up to bed but she said she would only go if Daddy would take her up to bed and say prayers with her. This had never happened before. Her father, very moved by this, took her upstairs. From that moment on, even the police noticed a new peace and calm in the area.


# Russia with Love


In the middle of a June night in 1987 I was woken by a phone call from a friend, a Franciscan in New York. He had just succeeded in tracing me to the Australian city where I was staying. He was full of the thoughts and ideas which he and his friends had been discussing 'We have just realised,' he said, 'that, on the Eastern front during the war, twenty-one million Russians died. They were our allies; they fought for our freedom and yet no one has mourned them or committed them to God. These, along with the three million more who died during the Stalin era, are the lost who still haunt the corridors of the Kremlin. They cry out in their pain; in their neglect; in their anger and fear. The rulers of Russia are possessed by these spirits so they too are angry and afraid. And they think, mistakenly, that it is the West

84

which threatens them.' My Franciscan friend invited me to join them in prayer for these people at a Eucharist.

It is true that in Moscow there are graveyards with rows of crosses but these represent only a fraction of the total number of their war dead. And how few Russians would have known how to mourn them; how to apologise to God or how to commit them in love to Him. The threat to Russia comes from within for who would ever wish to take over that vast array of divided nations?

In the churches of Australia we began to pray as our friends had asked us to and during these services people had visions of thousands of people in the far distance rising out of darkness into a warm light. And in the following months this prayer was taken up by churches in Canada, America and Britain. It was during this time that we heard of the German youth's flight in his light plane into Red Square and, although we knew he had been planning this for months, we took it as a sign of peace.

Can we hope that our prayers can lighten the load which President Gorbachev now carries? Through them we can, at least, express our gratitude to God for those who died for us.


# The Island


The family had always camped on the island. Every weekend throughout the summer months, they had come by car and then boat to set up their tents before combing the beach for dry wood for their fire. They looked on the island as their own possession; no one else ever landed on it, though many boats passed by, and they knew every tree stump and rocky outcrop from which they would spend many dreamy hours fishing.

Everyone slept soundly on the island until one summer when the father began to wake up frequently, disturbed as he first thought by the flap of a small piece of canvas or the falling of a twig. As soon as he dropped off to sleep again, something would again wake him. He tried staying awake in the hope of catching whatever it was. He now thought it might be a chipmunk or squirrel although they had never seen these animals on the island in the daytime.

As time went by, the nightly disturbances became more intrusive and occurred with greater regularity. He began to worry because his holidays on the island were not giving him the rest which he needed and expected.

One evening I was visiting him with some friends and he told us about his trouble. I asked him about the history of the island and he told me that the area had been inhabited by Indian tribes for centuries until the French settlers had fought and overrun them regardless of ownership. Later they had paid one tribe to fight another. Rotting wood stumps and disturbed earth probably marked the site of graveyards for some of those killed. There must have been many others killed in isolated places, caught perhaps while sleeping, their position given away by their camp fires.

It seemed to me unlikely in that unmapped, isolated area, that a priest would ever have been available. Many therefore could have died, unmourned and uncommitted. If it was these unmourned deaths, which were accounting for the disturbances, I wondered why it was only now that someone should be sensitive to them? He then told me that a year earlier, he had read my book, *Healing the Family Tree*, and that this had opened his mind to the problem of the unmourned dead, but he had not consciously associated this with the Island. Was it possible that with his new sensitivity to such things, the dead now felt this was someone to whom they could reveal their plight; someone who might bring them help? We decided to pray along these lines and to ask a

86

priest to carry some holy water or the reserved sacrament on his next visit to the island. A service was then held on the island and the disturbances stopped.

Many questions are raised by this story. Do the dead only haunt people they trust? Do they wait for a sensitive person? In this case, did they wait until this man understood their plight? Were they wandering the face of the earth or were they limited to this one place where they died? Was the disturbance only seasonal, corresponding to the time of their death? Certainly, we didn't know whether it was one person or many people so we could only guess that it might be a white man who had sinned; had killed others and was earthbound, no one having mourned his death or prayed for him.

Was the peace which followed the service sufficient proof that the dead had been released or was it one man's form of brain-washing? Certainly, the rest of the family had not been aware of what he was experiencing until our discussions with him.


# Camp Douglas


The origin of the American Civil War lay in the fact that the Southern States shipped raw materials to England where manufacturing was cheaper than in the Northern States. The South would then buy back England's exports at a lower price than the North would charge. The question of slave ownership in the South was the one overtly blamed as the righteous cause of the fighting.

One of the recruiting centres for the North American Union army was outside Chicago on land owned by a very wealthy citizen named Douglas. During the Civil War both sides took prisoners, many finding themselves prisoners of their own brothers. Prison camps had to be set up and the recruiting centre, Camp Douglas, was used for this purpose. Wooden huts were hastily erected and the prisoners herded into them. During the four years' war, 32,000 prisoners were housed there and 6000 of them died.

A psychiatrist, of my acquaintance, began further research searching through maps and drawings and also on site explorations, and discovered that the North had concealed the truth about the prison conditions. One of the reports he studied was by Henry Stanley, later famous for his adventures in Africa when searching for David Livingstone. He, himself, had been a prisoner in Camp Douglas and tells of the construction of walls fourteen feet high and of a white line drawn fifty feet from the wall beyond which no prisoner could go: the penalty for doing so was death. Stanley wrote of 'Gophers', prisoners who attempted to tunnel their way out, and of shootings and torture that occurred there. Men would be tied up by their thumbs so that only their toes touched the ground. Some were bound to crosses with their arms outstretched, others had large cannon balls chained to their ankles. Typhus, smallpox and dysentery were the biggest killers and the corpses were slung onto carts for the daily delivery to a mass grave at Oakwood. The city of Chicago refused to supply medicines or materials for a sewage system.

In 1986 I visited Chicago and met a man, who had suffered for years from intense pain in his thighs and crutch and up his shoulder on the left side. As we talked about all that had occurred at Camp Douglas, he realised that his pain matched exactly that which the prisoners would have felt, many of whom died as a result. Their feet had been tied to weights high above the ground, their hands tied behind their backs and a narrow plank in the crutch their only support until they died. This man, and a number of other Chicago residents who sensed that the guilt of their ancestors still lay on their shoulders, decided to hold a Mass of the Resurrection. The service was held on a sunny August afternoon on the grass beside the Oakwood Cemetery Memorial which had been erected later by Southerners. On the memorial are 6000 names and the graves of the Northern guards are nearby. Also nearby are the graves of the Northern dead.

Representatives of all walks of life came to the service and prayers took the form of proxy confession and apologies to God through Christ. A priest apologised for the lack of burial and committal services in the 1860's. A man, who had experienced prison life during World War II, prayed for those who, though heroes in their own land, had been plunged into despair at finding themselves nobodies – cut off from their own families, starving and filthy. His prayer was, 'Allow them, Lord, now to know that there is love and forgiveness and to be united with their loved ones on the heavenly pathway.' A housewife prayed for those whose home life had been destroyed and for the children who had grown up without fathers. A business man prayed for those who had exploited the situation and gained financially from the timber and food supplies. A city official prayed for the meanness of the city which was required to spend a million dollars a month on food begrudged thirty eight thousand for a sewage system. A doctor apologised for the deliberate withholding of medical supplies and the unwillingness of professional people to help the prisoners. A lady prayed for the 'ladies' of the time who would climb on a specially built platform from whence they could 'look down' on 'the enemy'. And another man prayed for the men who, in their callous greed, had built the platform and collected the money.

Amongst us was a well-known man whose great-uncle had been captain of a river boat and who after the war in

1865, had been ordered to ship 800 prisoners up the Missis-sippi. He had packed them in the boat and battened down the hatches. Confederate guards then came aboard and, standing along one side of the boat, they overloaded it and tipped it over drowning all eight hundred prisoners. The guards and the captain swam safely ashore. All this hap-pened within sight of the embarkation jetty and the captain was hailed as a hero by the Southerners.

The captain's descendant felt the burden of his great uncle's guilt very heavily and at the service he voiced his repentance and prayed for all those who had drowned in the incident. During the prayers many had visions of the prison-ers, dirty and dishevelled, still crawling on their hands and knees to the altar; and visions of other graves in the cemetery being opened, and also of families reunited in heaven.

One immediate and unexpected result of this service was the complete release from pain of the young man who had consulted me earlier. And two years after this service was held he telephoned me to say that he had remained well and pain-free and wanted to express his gratitude.

# Obstetrics and Gynaecology

On starting a new hospital job in obstetrics and gynaecology a young lady doctor moved into a modern hospital flat. It had a good atmosphere and was completely self-contained. However, every night she was woken by the figure of a man standing near her bed and watching her. She tried leaving a light on all night but his presence still persisted. She was constantly woken up by him and consequently became very tired and distressed.

One night, when she was on duty, she was talking to the

night sister who, without knowing of her problem, told her of a young doctor who had committed suicide while living in that block of flats. On coming off duty she immediately telephoned her mother who lived twenty miles away. They decided that they would show forth the bread and wine in their homes and ask forgiveness on behalf of the man for having taken his life and apologise for the pressures he had obviously been suffering.

Young doctors are put under enormous pressure to assist in abortions and even if they refuse they still have in their care patients, who are awaiting, or have just had, abortions; so they are aware of the large numbers that take place. Since it was possible that this might have been a contributing reason for this doctors suicide, mother and daughter agreed to 'apologise' for all the abortions that had taken place in the hospital; and pray for all the babies lost through miscarriages, too premature to warrant a proper burial according to the present hospital rules. As soon as the apologies for the young doctor were made the mother saw the figure of a young man wearing the long white coat of a hospital doctor leaning on the shoulder of Our Lord and weeping. As soon as the miscarried babies were prayed for the room almost overflowed with babies and infants, smiling, gurgling and sounding and looking so happy and contented that the mother could not stop tears of pure joy from running down her cheeks. Their presence and movement seemed to last for several minutes and then they gradually disappeared into the light. There were so many they seemed to be everywhere. It was as if someone had just exploded a feather pillow in the air and instead of feathers everywhere there were babies.

From that moment on the young doctor's presence was never again felt or seen and the young lady was able to sleep in peace.

# The Healing Eucharist

Provoked by a clergyman's remark that The Eucharist will be celebrated as usual I responded that it is never usual if we celebrate it as our Lord intended. Every time we celebrate the Eucharist we should experience a fresh awakening of our senses enabling us to see and hear and experience the eternal world around us. We should catch a glimpse of happenings 'through the veil'. We have the privilege of 'shewing forth His death', (1 Cor.11.26) and demonstrating 'unto the principalities and powers . . . by the church, and manifold wisdom of God'. (Ephes.3.10).

We often tend to be too self-centred in our view of the Eucharist, concerned only with what is in it for us. Christ said, 'This is My blood of the new covenant, shed for you and for many for the remission of sins.' (Book of Common Prayer). Too often we fail to realise the full implications of this word 'many'. We are responsible for 'showing forth' to our own generation: for keeping the Eucharist alive in the fullness of its meaning. But we are also responsible for those who have died. We can, as it were, stand proxy for them in the Eucharist, in confession, and in committal: 'to this end Christ both died and rose . . . that He might be Lord both of the dead and living'. (Romans 14.9). Who are we to limit His activity?

Peter, in his first letter, describes Jesus as having gone to preach to the dead after His crucifixion. (1 Peter 3.19). He repeats this in the following chapter (1 Peter 4.6) but there the word 'preach' should be translated 'evangelise'. Paul, in his first letter to the Corinthians, refers to the apparently common practice of Christians being baptised on behalf of their dead and asks why they are doing it. Here Paul is emphasising the reality of life after death and he clearly approves of taking responsibility for the dead. Bishop Cuthbert Bardsley, interpreted this by saying that in the Eucharist we are 'immersing the dead into Christ's salvation'.

The writer of the Hebrews speaks of the great cloud of those who have gone before witnessing what we do. (Hebrews 12.1). I am told by theologians that Hebrews 12 should not have been separated from Hebrews 11 for the last words in verse 40 are, 'they without us cannot be made perfect' and one of the possible interpretations is that we who are alive still have volition and can be responsible for those who never had a chance.

Questions arise here because of the sentence in Hebrews which says, 'now once in the end of the world hath He appeared to put away sin by the sacrifice of Himself. And as it is appointed unto men once to die but after that the judgment, so Christ was once offered to bear the sins of many'. (Hebrews 9.26–28). The question we must ask is whether a man is judged at the moment he comes face to face with the truth about God and the truth about himself: whether this happens before or after physical death. As Jesus Himself said, 'He that heareth My word and believeth on Him that sent Me, hath everlasting life, and shall not come into condemnation; but is passed from death into life'. (John 5.24).

Life does not come to a standstill after physical death. The learning process must go on. We are only too aware of how little we know and understand. And as life goes on, then the need for responsible prayer must also go on.

At a Eucharistic service held either on behalf of the dead or to release someone held in bondage to the dead, we should only think of the service being one per cent for our own benefit and for the healing of our hurts and memories:

but ninety-nine per cent for the benefit of the one who has died and in addition for those who, for some reason, have died unmourned: the miscarried; the stillborn; the aborted babies; the war dead; those who went missing and have no known burial place; the suicides; those who have never had the opportunity to know God's love and forgiveness; and those who died before they could put right things that were wrong in their life on earth.

At a Eucharist service we should always begin with the Lord's prayer. He is saying it with us while we, for our part, are welcoming His presence. He is clearing our relationship with God as we forgive those who have hurt us. Having received His forgiveness for ourselves we then have the right, as we say the last line of the prayer, to dismiss Satan and his minions in Christ's Name.

Before saying our confession and receiving absolution, we should set aside time to look at our own wrong-doing and to confess the sins of the dead for whom we are holding the service. Confession is best said aloud as it helps to make it a fully conscious act. It also helps the disturbed person to see their problem objectively; he or she can relate their own symptoms to the dead person's needs or to the circumstances in which death occurred.

Suggested readings during the Eucharist service are:
Ephesians 6.12; and 3 7–19.
St John 5 24–29.
The responses should read:
Christ has died.
Christ has risen.
Christ *has* come again.

The 'comfortable words' used in the liturgy, refer to *all* generations of the world: to *all* men. When reading the first epistle of St John (2.2) the whole verse should be read including, 'And He is the propitiation for our sins: and not for ours only but also for the sins of the whole world.' This broadens our own responsibility.

As we receive the bread, let us look at it and realize that through it Christ is touching us. It is His life, representing all that He did, taught and preached. We feel His rejection; His betrayal; His torture; and His death. By taking this into ourselves, we are healed.

As we receive the cup we accept the washing away of our guilt and the stains of sin; and with thanksgiving, we receive salvation.

As we receive Communion, we can picture, often vividly, the dead for whom we pray, brought to us by the angels to share the service with us and to witness what we do. Then we can see them, as Heaven opens for them, starting on their new journey, now clothed in white. (Revelation 7 9–17). At the same time, those who have been bound, haunted, or possessed by these earth-bound souls, find freedom to become the people God intends them to be.

At this service, hundreds of patients, diagnosed as suffering from epilepsy, schizophrenia, anorexia nervosa or bulimia, have been freed from illness, as also have people suffering from diabetes, multiple sclerosis and other physical conditions thought to be incurable.

That the unfinished business of an ancestor may bring trouble to his descendants, was well recognised in the Old Testament. In Exodus (20.5) God says through Moses, 'I am a jealous God visiting the iniquity of the fathers upon the children unto the third and fourth generation of those who hate Me'. A straightforward public health observation of transmitted disease! The same words are quoted again in Exodus (34, 7) and Numbers (16. 18).

But also in the Old Testament comes the promise of release. In Ezekiel (18, 2) the Lord says, 'What mean ye that ye use the proverb concerning the land of Israel, the fathers have eaten sour grapes and children's teeth are set on edge?' 'As I live', saith the Lord, 'ye shall not have occasion any more to use this proverb'. Release will come with individual repentance.

In our efforts to help the dead, our Lord has given us a precedent in the story of the raising of Lazarus:

Jesus is told of the illness of Lazarus.

He is asked to come.

He is told of Lazarus' death.

He is taken to the tomb.

He tells the family to roll away the stone over the entrance.

He tells the family to unbind Lazarus.

Jesus Christ stood by all the time.

In our prayers, we too have to 'roll away the stone' and uncover all the secrets of the past. And we must always be *specific*. The immediate family should also be involved if possible. Then we can expect to see results in healing and liberation.

What happens to people of other faiths? Jews, Hindus, Parsees, Buddhists as well as avowed atheists – who after reading my first book *Healing the Family Tree*, have attended a Eucharistic service for their families and at the service have seen the Lord, have seen the dead rise to heaven; and have witnessed healings? Bishop Morris Maddox, adviser on healing to the Archbishop of Canterbury, commented, 'Here you have found a lacuna [gap] in the healing through the Church and medicine and filled it.'

This chapter is written as a challenge to you personally, to draw your own Family Tree and to talk to God about the people on it; to play your part and where necessary to bring redemption and healing for the sins and traumas of the past.

*Also Published by Darley Anderson*

# The Moon Looks Down
## KENNETH AND
## FRANCES McALL

Kenneth and Frances McAll were married in Peking in 1940 at a time of constant skirmishing between Chinese and Japanese forces. By 1941, in the turmoil of the Second World War, destitute and homeless they were imprisoned by the Japanese with their baby daughter. Over the next four years, they were moved from one interment camp to another, learning lessons in human behaviour, which stood them in good stead when they were held in a condemned Shanghai warehouse with 1200 other people.

During these years, Kenneth, who had learned his skills from a badly wounded Chinese guerilla, kept a record of their lives in drawings done with brush and ink. And for some of this time Eric Liddell, the famous Olympic runner, worked closely with him.

Written by his wife this unique and inspiring personal record documents their gruelling experiences in the Japanese internment camps and tells the story of a well-organised, contented community with faith in the future which emerged against this backdrop of squalor and hardship.

The First Edition of this unique book has 75 full page illustrations; 10 half page illustrations and a beautiful full colour Frontispiece. It is a collectors item.

**The Moon Looks Down** can be ordered direct by post in the U.K.

Cheques payable to DARLEY ANDERSON for the cost

of the book (£24.95 per copy) plus postage: £2.10 for the first book and £1.00 for each additional book ordered. And send to: Darley Anderson Bookservice by Post, 11 Eustace Road, London SW6 1JB.

Postage rates are subject to revision.

# The Garden of the Beloved
## ROBERT WAY

**The beautifully written and original story of a rich young man who seeks to learn the art of loving from a humble gardener who tends the Garden of the Beloved.**

'It is a subject on which so much has been written before. Yet Robert Way has, I am sure, caught with a few words the essential truth with an insight akin to the great classical works on the subject.'

*Delia Smith*

'. . . A book of genius, akin to Kahil Gibran's THE PROPHET, which is likely to become a classic. It's fascinating, humbling and inspiring.'

*FK Bulletin*

'It is short . . . it is simple, and it is beautifully written. In my opinion it is superb – and I do not say that lightly.'
*East Anglian Daily Times*

'I found it a book of sheer delight . . . It was pure pleasure to read, and with its timeless style I have no doubt that it will become a worldwide classic.'

*David Watson*

'Easy to read, simple and profound.'

*The Old Lady of Threadneedle Street*

'A really delightful book.'

*Colin Cowdrey*

'A work of distinction that will endure.'

*Robert Dougall*

'The Garden of the Beloved will become a new semi-religious bestseller.'

*Daily Telegraph*

'The language in which it is told is deceptively simple, poignantly impressive.'

*The Bookseller*

'To be read, re-read and to be pondered, for the gentle simplicity of the narrative covers a depth and profundity rarely met with today.'

*The Middle Way*

'. . . it will prove to be comforting and inspiring to those who read it.'

*Christian Herald*

'With consummate artistry and simplicity, Robert Way has given us a book, superbly illustrated, which can be read and re-read again.'

*British Weekly*

'A book with unique qualities.'

*Trevor Huddleston*

'*The Garden of the Beloved* is a very gentle book. It is well produced, nice to handle, with plenty of space.'

*Way of Life*

'A rare and precious book.'

*The Life of Faith*

'I was very interested to read it and found it very good.'

*Barbara Cartland*

'. . . simple, fascinating and spiritually inspiring.'

*Catholic Herald*

'I have now read The Garden of the Beloved and enjoyed it very much.'

*Cardinal Hume*

'. . . uncommonly well written.'

*Financial Times*

'I am sure that many people will find this book attractive and browsing through it will discover helpful ideas in its pages.'

*Archbishop Bruno Heim*

**The Garden of the Beloved** can be ordered direct by post in the UK.

Cheques payable to DARLEY ANDERSON for the cost of the book (£3.99 per copy) plus postage: 50p for the first book and 30p for each additional book ordered. And send to: Darley Anderson, Bookservice by Post, 11 Eustace Road, London SW1 1JB.

Darley Anderson reserves the right if necessary to increase this retail price in future printings. Postage rates are also subject to revision.

# The Wisdom of the Desert
## THOMAS MERTON

**The ancient hermits were holy men. They rejected the bogus conformity of the world and sought true freedom in the deserts of Egypt and Palestine. They had much in common with Zen Buddhist monks and Indian yogis. Many came to them for advice and their sayings were remembered, passed on and written down.**

**Their wisdom was simple, practical and timeless.**

'I loved the Wisdom of the Desert but to ask me for a few words of commendation on the sayings of the elders is like a request to dance in front of Dame Margot or sing to Caruso in his bath.'

*Auberon Waugh*

'Merton believed as I do, that "we need to learn from these men of the Fourth Century".'

*Kenneth Leech*

'A remarkable collection. Merton is always compulsively readable.'

*The Universe*

'In the age of affluence the value of the lives of holy men can still be recognised.'

*The Times*

'We cannot all retire to the desert in solitude to weave baskets and pray but from these monks we can learn something of the basic realities of the interior life which are valid for all ages.'

*Sean Fagan SM*

'Every time we return to these timeless sayings we are sure to meet a pearl.'

*Frederick Hockey OSB*

'His prose is a delight to read.'

*The Evangelical Quarterly*

'Full of marvellous things.'

*BBC Radio Medway*

'Superb material for contemplating, for daily reflection and thoughts wherever we are. A most timely, gentle book.'

*World Faiths*

'. . . selective in his choice of the sayings so that the 150 of this collection are pearls.'

*Church Scene (Australia)*

'A delightful book full of humour as well as wisdom.'

*The Franciscan*

**The Wisdom of the Desert** can be ordered direct by post in the UK.

Cheques payable to Darley Anderson for the cost of the book (£3.50 per copy) plus postage: 50p for the first book and 30p for each additional book ordered. And send to: Darley Anderson, Bookservice by Post, 11 Eustace Road, London SW6 1JB.

Darley Anderson reserves the right if necessary to increase this retail price in future printings. Postage rates are also subject to revision.